THE SCOTTISH PARLIAMENT

AN INTRODUCTION

THE SCOTTISH PARLIAMENT

AN INTRODUCTION

Jean McFadden

Senior Lecturer in Law, University of Strathclyde

Mark Lazarowicz

Member of Parliament, Advocate

Print on Demand Edition

Tottel
publishing

Published by
Tottel Publishing Ltd
Maxwelton House
41-43 Boltro Road
Haywards Heath
West Sussex
RH16 1BJ

Tottel Publishing Ltd
9-10 St Andrew Square
Edinburgh
EH2 2AF

ISBN 13: 978-1-84592-384-6
ISBN 10: 1-84592-384-7
© Reed Elsevier (UK) Ltd 2003
First published by T&T Clark 1999
Second edition 2000
Third edition published by LexisNexis 2003
Formerly published by LexisNexis Butterworths

This edition reprinted by Tottel Publishing Ltd 2006

British Library Cataloguing-in-Publication Data.
A catalogue record for this book is available from the British Library.

Typeset by Phoenix Photosetting, Chatham, Kent
Printed and bound in Great Britain by
CPI Antony Rowe, Eastbourne, East Sussex

PREFACE

It used to be said that what distinguished the British political system from practically every other country in the world was the absence of a written constitution. The extent to which that statement is true has become significantly smaller in the last 30 years, as a result of the UK joining the European Community and becoming bound by the Treaty of Rome and its successors. Now the combined effect of the Human Rights Act 1998 and the Scotland Act 1998, when added to the European treaties, means that in Scotland the rights of individuals and the powers of the state are, to a considerable extent, based on fundamental constitutional laws which together can truly be said to be the written constitution of Scotland.

This book aims to be a concise, but comprehensive, guide to that part of the Scottish constitution which is based on the Scotland Act 1998. It seeks to place the constitutional settlement which that Act represents in its historical setting, as well as the internal context of the Scottish Parliament's relations with local government and other public bodies, and the external context of its relations with the Westminster Parliament and Europe. The procedures and internal working arrangements of the Parliament are also considered.

This new edition takes account of the results of the second ordinary election to the Scottish Parliament and the forming of the new Scottish Administration in May 2003. It also brings the reader up-to-date on various other constitutional changes which have occurred since 2000.

The authors wish to thank William Bain, Arnold Bell, Kenneth Campbell, David Johnston, and Patricia Hogg for helpful comments on the text. They would also like to thank Alan Barr, Lynda Clark, QC, MP, and Neil Davidson, QC for advice on some particular issues considered in the book. Thanks are also due to the staff of the Scottish Parliament for helpful advice on a number of factual matters concerning the operation of the Parliament. Jean McFadden expresses her thanks to Dale McFadzean for teaching her time-saving tricks on the computer, to Chris Nicholson for invaluable research assistance and to Kitty Bell, June Davidson, Linda Hamilton and Ian Tully of Glasgow City Council for help on various issues. Thanks also to Andrew Mylne, Head of the Legislation Team in the Scottish Parliament, for helpful comments on chapter 5. Tables 5.1 and 5.2 are reproduced by permission of the Scottish Parliament. The authors, of course, accept full responsibility for any errors and omissions.

The authors acknowledge the permission given by Her Majesty's Stationery Office to reproduce the map on page 111.

Jean McFadden
Mark Lazarowicz
August 2003

CONTENTS

1 THE SCOTTISH PARLIAMENT: THE BACKGROUND

INTRODUCTION

The Scotland Act 1998[1] was one of the most important constitutional statutes passed by the UK Parliament for a very long time, with great significance for the rest of the UK as well as for Scotland. In Scottish terms, it established a parliament which has the powers to make laws for Scotland in a wide range of areas. In UK terms, it should be seen as an important element in a wider package of devolutionary or decentralising measures which have so far included a National Assembly for Wales, with mainly administrative powers, and an Assembly in Northern Ireland, with legislative powers. The establishment of these institutions represents a significant transfer of power from the UK Parliament and may in time lead to the establishment of regional assemblies in England.

SCOTLAND AND THE UNION[2]

Prior to 1707, England and Scotland possessed separate constitutions and parliaments. Scotland and England came together in a political union in 1707 after the Parliaments of England and Scotland passed individual Acts of Union whereby the separate Parliaments of the two countries ceased to exist and were replaced by the Parliament of the United Kingdom of Great Britain. Although the Scottish Parliament was abolished in 1707, the Scots maintained a sense of national identity due, in part, to the fact that the Presbyterian Church and the Scottish legal system were preserved by the terms of the Union. The union was not warmly embraced by most Scots. Indeed, there was rioting on the streets of Glasgow and Edinburgh when the terms were first made public. However, the economic situation at the time was such that acceptance of the union was almost inevitable and it was largely tolerated. The arrangements for the government of Scotland from London were, for much of the eighteenth and nineteenth centuries, in the hands of the Lord Advocate, a Law Officer appointed by the government. Interest in parliamentary affairs by Scots was minimal as their MPs were manipulated to dance to the government's tune. The electoral system was so corrupt and the number of people entitled to vote so tiny that not even the Scottish aristocracy, let alone the ordinary Scot, could hope to achieve influence. In 1823 it was estimated that fewer than 3,000 men were entitled to vote. (Women were not to get the vote until 1918). However, demand for electoral reform grew and, in 1832, the male middle classes were enfranchised by the Representation of the

---

[1] All references in this book to sections and Schedules which do not specify the legislation concerned are references to the Scotland Act 1998.

[2] For further reading on the political and historical background, see the books by Alice Brown et al, Michael Fry, and James Kellas, in the list of 'Further Reading' at the end of this book.

People (Scotland) Act, followed by the Representation of the People Acts of 1867 and 1884 which extended the franchise to include all men aged 21 years or over. As more and more men were given the vote, discontent rose about the lack of interest shown by the Westminster Parliament in Scottish affairs.

THE ROAD TO DEVOLUTION

Demand grew for the appointment of a Scottish Secretary of State, a post which had been abolished in 1746. In 1885, the government passed the Secretary for Scotland Act which established the post of Secretary for Scotland and the Scottish Office, based in Dover House in London. In 1926, the post was upgraded to that of Secretary of State and in 1939 the Scottish Office was moved to St Andrew's House in Edinburgh. The Secretary of State for Scotland has had a seat in the Cabinet in peacetime since 1892.

A number of factors, including the rise of the Irish Home Rule movement in the nineteenth century, led to the emergence of a Scottish Home Rule Association in 1886. Scottish home rule was frequently discussed in the House of Commons although no Bill reached the statute book to provide a parliament for Scotland, similar to that which was provided for Northern Ireland by the Government of Ireland Act 1920.

The National Party for Scotland was founded in 1928 and started to contest elections in the following year. In 1934, the National Party of Scotland merged with another home rule party, the Scottish Party, to form the Scottish National Party (SNP). The SNP won its first parliamentary seat in a by-election in Motherwell in 1945 but lost it in the general election later that year. The SNP made no more headway in terms of parliamentary seats for over 20 years but gained an increasing number of votes, particularly in by-elections. In 1967, they won the previously safe Labour seat of Hamilton in a by-election and in the following year they won 30 per cent of the vote and 108 seats in the local government elections.

The Labour Government, concerned by the electoral success of the SNP and of the Welsh nationalist party, Plaid Cymru, which had won a Welsh by-election in 1966, appointed, in 1969, a Royal Commission (chaired by Lord Crowther and after his death by Lord Kilbrandon) to examine the constitution of the UK. The Commission reported in 1973[3]. It rejected separatism and federalism as solutions and recommended a directly elected assembly for Scotland, elected on the system of the single transferable vote. The response to the Commission's report by the Conservative and Labour Parties was lukewarm and neither party included devolution in their manifestos for the general election which was held in February 1974. The results of that election, however, gave devolution a new lease of life as the SNP won seven seats and Plaid Cymru two seats.

The new Labour Government, which did not have an outright majority of seats in the House of Commons, was forced to make concessions to the nationalist parties and announced that it would bring forward proposals for consideration. In September 1974, a White Paper was published entitled *Democracy and Devolution: Proposals for Scotland and Wales*[4]. It proposed directly elected

---

[3] Cmnd 5460.
[4] Cmnd 5732.

assemblies for Scotland and Wales, with the Scottish Assembly having legislative, but not tax-raising, powers and the Welsh Assembly having executive powers only. A further general election was held in October 1974 at which the SNP won 11 seats. A second White Paper was published in November 1975 entitled *Our Changing Democracy: Devolution to Scotland and Wales*[5]. A Scotland and Wales Bill was published in November 1976 but the government, lacking a secure majority, was unable to get it through all the necessary stages in Parliament and the Bill was dropped. The following year, separate Bills for Scotland and Wales were introduced. During the parliamentary process an amendment was introduced which made it necessary for 40 per cent of the electorates to vote 'Yes' in referenda before the Acts could be brought into operation. The Scotland and the Wales Acts received the Royal Assent in 1978 and the referenda were held in March 1979. Although the majority of Scots who did vote voted 'Yes', the 40 per cent threshold was not reached. The Welsh decisively voted 'No'. A motion of no confidence in the Labour Government was tabled, the government was defeated and a general election was held in May 1979 which was won by the Conservatives under Margaret Thatcher. The Scotland and the Wales Acts were repealed in the following month.

THE SCOTTISH CONSTITUTIONAL CONVENTION

The Conservative Government remained in power for 18 years and was implacably opposed to devolution but the desire for some form of devolution in Scotland remained and a cross-party Campaign for a Scottish Assembly (CSA) was formed in 1980. Following the re-election of the Conservatives in 1983 and 1987, the CSA set up a committee of prominent Scots who produced *The Claim of Right for Scotland* in 1988 which advocated the establishment of a constitutional convention to draw up plans for Scottish self-government. The Scottish Constitutional Convention (SCC) was set up in March 1989 with the involvement of the Labour and Liberal Parties and several smaller parties, but without the Conservatives and the SNP. Also in membership were most of the Scottish local authorities and representatives of a wide spectrum of Scottish life. The SCC published a number of documents culminating in *Scotland's Parliament: Scotland's Right* (November 1995) which advocated a Scottish Parliament elected partly by the traditional 'first past the post' system and partly by a form of proportional representation. The SCC recommended that the Parliament should have legislative powers over a wide range of domestic issues and the power to vary income tax by up to 3p in the pound.

THE 1997 GENERAL ELECTION AND THE REFERENDUM

The Labour Party and the Liberal Democrat Party included a commitment to a Scottish Parliament, based on the proposals of the SCC, in their manifestos for the 1997 General Election. The Labour Party won that election with a very large majority and within three months published a White Paper, *Scotland's Parliament*[6], which detailed their plans for a devolved parliament with legislative

---

[5] Cmnd 6348.
[6] Cm. 3658.

and limited tax-varying powers. Before introducing a Bill to establish the parliament, the government wanted the proposal to be endorsed by the Scottish people in a referendum. The Referendums Act 1997 was quickly passed by the UK Parliament and a referendum was held in September 1997. The electorate had to vote on two issues – on the principle of a Scottish Parliament, and on its tax-varying powers. The answers which the Scottish people gave to both questions were emphatically in the affirmative. On the issue of a Scottish Parliament, 74.3 per cent of those who did vote voted 'Yes' (a total of 1,775,045 voters). On the issue of tax-varying powers, 63.5 per cent voted 'Yes' (1,512,889 voters).

The government introduced the Scotland Bill into the House of Commons in December 1997. The Bill received the Royal Assent on 19 November 1998. The first general election to the Scottish Parliament was held on 6 May 1999. The Parliament was formally opened by the Queen on 1 July 1999 and on that date the Parliament assumed its full powers. After extended negotiations following that general election, the Scottish Labour and Liberal Democrat Parties formed a coalition administration with the backing of 73 of the 129 members of the Parliament. That coalition continued in office until the second Scottish parliamentary general election on 1 May 2003, and resumed the administration thereafter (although this time with a slim combined overall majority of five seats, as a a result of a decline in support for the coalition's larger party, the Labour Party).

The following chapters deal with various aspects of the Scottish Parliament, including elections, the powers of the Parliament, and how it goes about its business. The Scottish Government and the powers of the First Minister and other Ministers are examined, as are relations with the UK Parliament and how legal disputes and challenges to the powers of the Parliament and Executive are resolved. The vital area of financing the Parliament is also examined. Finally, there is discussion of the relationships between the Parliament and local government and the Parliament and Europe.

2 THE POWERS OF THE PARLIAMENT

INTRODUCTION

The form of government which the establishment of a Scottish Parliament brings to Scotland is known as legislative devolution. This means that the UK Parliament has voluntarily transferred a number of its law-making powers to the Scottish Parliament without relinquishing its own supreme authority or sovereignty. The Scottish Parliament is not independent. It is not free to make laws in any area which it chooses. Therefore, there has to be a framework which defines the areas in which it has the power to make laws (its legislative competence) and those areas where the UK Parliament has not relinquished its law-making power. We must, then, examine how the UK Parliament has gone about setting that framework. We must also consider the impact of the legal doctrine known as the sovereignty of Parliament.

THE DIVISION OF POWERS – TWO BASIC MODELS

In any system of government where powers are divided between two levels – central and regional, state or provincial – the possibility of one level of government trespassing into the legislative or executive territory of the other may arise. Therefore, the powers of each must be set out in a written document. In the vast majority of countries this document will be the constitution. However, since the UK does not have a constitution contained in one single document the powers of the two levels of government are set out in an Act of Parliament. In the case of Scotland, the Act of Parliament is the Scotland Act 1998 (SA 1998).

Broadly speaking, there are two basic models for the constitution or the Act of Parliament to follow:

- the central authority devolves all of its powers to the local or subordinate body except for certain powers which it specifically reserves to itself;
- the central authority devolves to the local or subordinate body certain specified powers while everything not so specified is, by implication, reserved to the centre.

The former is called the retaining model, and the latter the transferring model. Put simply, the retaining model spells out what the subordinate or local body *cannot* do and it is implied that it *can* do everything not spelled out. The transferring model spells out what the local or subordinate body *can* do and it is implied that it *cannot* do anything which is not mentioned.

The American Constitution is an example of the retaining model. The powers of the United States Congress (the federal or central legislature) are set out in Article 1. The powers of the states, known as 'residuary' powers are set out in the Tenth Amendment to the Constitution as follows: 'The powers not delegated to the United States by the Constitution, nor prohibited by it to the States, are reserved to the States respectively or to the people'. The American model thus tilts the balance, at least in theory, against the centre, as everything not specified in the Constitution lies within the powers of the individual states.

The Canadian Constitution is an example of the transferring model and was designed to produce a strong central government. Section 91 of the British North America Act 1867, now known as the Constitution Act 1867, allocates national powers to the central or federal Parliament, while s 92 allocates regional powers to the provincial legislatures. Section 91, however, also gives the federal Parliament the power 'to make laws for the peace, order and good government of Canada in relation to all matters not coming within the classes of subjects assigned exclusively to the Provinces . . .'.

The Scotland Act 1978 (SA 1978) which was to have established a Scottish Assembly in 1979 was an example of the transferring model, specifying in great detail the legislative and executive powers which were to be devolved from Westminster. Schedule 10 to the SA 1978 listed 25 groups of matters which were to be devolved matters and another 25 which were specifically not included in those groups. There then followed a lengthy list of Acts of Parliament, going back to the Anatomy Act of 1832, and an indication of the extent to which each Act was or was not included in the groups of devolved matters. Schedule 11 to the SA 1978 then listed the matters which were within the powers of the Scottish Executive but not within the law-making powers of the Scottish Assembly. Schedule 16 contained another lengthy list, this time of amendments of Acts of the UK Parliament. The SA 1978 was extremely complex, would have required frequent updating to take account of new and amended legislation, and would have led to many challenges in court as to whether the Assembly was acting outwith its powers (ultra vires).

Three pieces of legislation for Northern Ireland give examples of the retaining model: the Government of Ireland Act 1920, the Northern Ireland Constitution Act 1973, and the Northern Ireland Act 1998.

The Government of Ireland Act 1920 which established the Northern Ireland Parliament at Stormont listed, not the devolved powers, but the powers reserved to Westminster. Section 4 of the Act provides that:

> Subject to the provisions of this Act . . . the Parliament of Northern Ireland shall . . . have powers to make laws for the peace, order and good government of Northern Ireland with the following limitations . . . that they shall not have powers to make laws in respect of the following matters in particular, namely . . .

There follows a list of 14 areas reserved to Westminster including, among others, the Crown, the making of peace or war, and the armed forces.

The Northern Ireland Constitution Act 1973 established the short-lived Northern Ireland Assembly and the power-sharing executive (it lasted for the first five months of 1974). Section 4(1) of the Act states: 'Laws may be made for Northern Ireland by Measures of the Assembly'. Matters excepted from the law-making powers of the Assembly were listed in Schedule 2 to the Act and included, among others, the Crown, the armed forces, and international relations.

The Northern Ireland Act 1998 (NIA 1998) established the Northern Ireland Assembly following the Belfast 'Good Friday' agreement earlier that year. Once again, this gave the assembly the power to make laws in all areas which were not specifically excluded from its competence. Schedule 2 to the NIA 1998 lists 'excepted matters' which are permanently outside the competence of the Assembly, and Schedule 3 to the Act lists 'reserved matters', over which the Assembly may legislate, but only with the consent of the Secretary of State for Northern Ireland. Section 4(2) of the NIA 1998 also gives the Secretary of State the power to remove matters from the list of reserved matters so that the Assembly then has the power to legislate in such areas without his or her consent (and also to put matters concerning which legislation did not previously need his consent onto the list of reserved matters).

THE SCOTLAND ACT 1998

The Scottish Constitutional Convention, early on in its life, adopted the principle of the sovereignty of the Scottish people, which led it to favour the retaining form of constitution. In its first report, *Towards a Scottish Parliament*, it declared that 'The type of statute which sits most easily with that principle is the retaining one; it reflects a constitutional settlement in which the Scottish people, being sovereign, agree to the exercise of specified powers by Westminster but retain their sovereignty over all other matters.'[1] In its later reports, the issue was not explicitly addressed but it appears that the Scottish Constitutional Convention expected that any new Scotland Act would, like the SA 1978, list the powers and responsibilities to be devolved from Westminster on the grounds that the UK Parliament would be unwilling to adopt the form of the Government of Ireland Act 1920 in the mistaken belief that it might be giving away too much power.

The Constitution Unit examined the two forms and, in its report *Scotland's Parliament: Fundamentals for a New Scotland Act*,[2] recommended strongly that the best method of ensuring legal clarity as to the scope of devolution was to specify the powers to be retained by Westminster and devolve the remainder. It rejected the view that this was, of necessity, a more generous approach. The method is neutral. It is the length and complexity of the list of retained powers which determines the level of generosity.

The Scottish Office had the benefit of the work of both the Scottish Constitutional Convention and the Constitution Unit in drawing up the White Paper, *Scotland's Parliament*, and the Scotland Bill. Specific reference is made in the White Paper to the Northern Ireland model and the government opted for the retaining model in the Scotland Bill. All matters which are not specifically reserved to the UK Parliament are devolved to the Scottish Parliament. From all accounts, the Secretary of State for Scotland seems to have played his hand particularly skilfully in the Cabinet to ensure that this was the form of legislation adopted.

THE SCOTTISH PARLIAMENT AND THE SOVEREIGNTY OF THE UK PARLIAMENT

As far as law-making powers are concerned, the important parts of the SA 1998 are ss 28–30 and Sch 5, which lists the powers which are retained by, or reserved

---

[1] *Towards a Scottish Parliament* (1989) p 36.

[2] *Scotland's Parliament: Fundamentals for a New Scotland Act* (1996). The Constitution Unit is a research project, based in University College, London. It has published a number of reports dealing with issues of constitutional reform.

to, the UK Parliament. Schedule 4, which sets out various enactments protected from modification by the Scottish Parliament, is also significant. Before we examine these, however, mention should be made of the UK constitutional doctrine of the sovereignty of parliament. The sovereignty of the UK Parliament is perhaps the most important doctrine of constitutional law in the UK. In its absolute form it means that the UK Parliament is the one supreme law-making body in the UK and can, in theory, pass any law that it wishes. Its laws cannot be declared invalid even by the highest court in the land, the House of Lords. This is not the case in federal states such as the United States or Germany, where there is a written constitution and a supreme court which can strike down a law as invalid if it is in conflict with the constitution. The sovereignty of the UK Parliament has undoubtedly been modified by our membership of the European Communities but, as far as domestic or national law is concerned, the doctrine remains firmly in place. Thus, any parliament or assembly created by the UK Parliament is a sub-ordinate body. It is not independent nor is it co-ordinate with central government as in a federal system. It may not only be overruled by the UK Parliament, it may even be abolished by it. Of course, this is legal theory and account has to be taken of practical politics. If the Scottish Parliament remains a relatively popular institution, no government at Westminster would want to incur the wrath of the Scottish electorate by interfering with the Scottish Parliament without good cause.

THE LAW-MAKING POWERS OF THE PARLIAMENT

Bearing this in mind, let us examine the law-making powers of the Scottish Parliament. The powers are contained in the SA 1998, ss 28–30. Section 28 states that, subject to various exceptions in s 29, the Scottish Parliament has the power to make laws which will be known as Acts of the Scottish Parliament. Proposed Acts are known as Bills, as at Westminster, and once Bills have passed through the Parliamentary stages and received the Royal Assent they become Acts. However, the final subsection of s 28 states that the power of the Parliament of the UK to make laws for Scotland remains unaffected. This is an assertion of the sovereignty of the UK Parliament. The UK Parliament can, by passing an Act at Westminster, override or nullify any Act of the Scottish Parliament and if the Scottish Parliament refuses to pass an Act which the government at Westminster wishes it to pass, the UK Parliament will simply pass one for it. However, as long as there are good working relationships between the two Parliaments and goodwill on both sides, it is unlikely that the UK Parliament would wish to assert its sovereignty in this way.

As it is in the retaining form, the SA 1998 does not list the areas in which the Scottish Parliament has the power to legislate. Instead, it lists the areas in which it cannot legislate, some of which are found in s 29 and the remainder in Schs 4 and 5.

Section 29 sets out a number of areas where any attempt by the Scottish Parliament to make law would be invalid:

- it cannot pass a valid law any provision of which would form part of the law of any country or territory other than Scotland or confer or remove functions which are exercisable except in or as regards Scotland. While it is extremely unlikely that the Scottish Parliament would want to pass a law for, say, France or Indonesia, this is designed to prevent it legislating, presumably inadvertently, for any other part of the UK;

- it cannot pass a valid law any provision of which is incompatible with those parts of the European Convention on Human Rights which are given effect by the Human Rights Act 1998;
- it cannot pass a valid law any provision of which is incompatible with European Community law. Although relations with the European Community are reserved to the UK Parliament, the Scottish Parliament is responsible for observing and implementing the various obligations under Community law in relation to devolved matters;
- it cannot pass a valid law any provision of which would remove the Lord Advocate from his position as head of the systems of criminal prosecution and investigation of deaths in Scotland. This is one of various measures in the SA 1998 designed to protect the independence of the Scottish Law Officers;
- it cannot pass a valid law any provision of which relates to matters which are reserved to the UK Parliament. These provisions are listed in Sch 5 and are dealt with below;
- it cannot pass a valid law any provision of which modifies any of the enactments listed in Sch 4. These are also dealt with below.

Section 30 enables Schs 4 and 5 to be modified by a parliamentary order known as an Order in Council. This enables the UK Parliament to make changes to the contents of these Schedules without the necessity of passing another Act of Parliament.

RESERVED MATTERS

The matters reserved to the UK Parliament are areas into which the Scottish Parliament may not trespass. Any attempt to make law in any of these areas would be invalid. The Scottish Constitutional Convention recommended that the primary matters which should be retained by the UK Parliament should be defence, foreign affairs, immigration, nationality, social security policy, and central economic and fiscal responsibilities. The White Paper, *Scotland's Parliament*, added to the list the constitution of the UK, common markets for UK goods and services, employment legislation, the regulation of certain professions, transport safety and regulation, and a miscellany of other matters including the regulatory framework for broadcasting, abortion, and equality legislation. The general justification is that there are many matters which can be more effectively and beneficially handled on a UK basis.[3]

When translated into the SA 1998 the reserved matters are set out in considerable detail (18 pages) in Sch 5. The Schedule is divided into three parts: Part I dealing with what are called General Reservations, Part II dealing with Specific Reservations and Part III dealing with miscellaneous matters under General Provisions.

---

[3] Paragraph 3.2.

General Reservations Part I

1. Various aspects of the constitution of the UK are reserved. These are:

- the Crown, including succession to the Crown and a regency;
- the Union of the Kingdoms of Scotland and England;
- the Parliament of the United Kingdom;
- the continued existence of the High Court of Justiciary and the Court of Session.

Thus, it is not be open to the Scottish Parliament to restore the Stuarts to the throne and the eighteenth century Acts relating to the Hanoverian Protestant succession will continue to apply to the succession to the throne on the death or abdication of the present Queen unless the UK Parliament deems otherwise.[4] Nor will it be possible for the Scottish Parliament to declare Scotland independent even if a majority of MSPs are members of the Scottish National Party, as that would affect, among other things, the union of the kingdoms which took place in 1603. The continued existence of the Scottish Courts was guaranteed in the Acts of Union of 1707 and that is further confirmed by these reservations.

2. The aspects of foreign affairs which are reserved include:

- international relations with territories outside the UK, the European Communities and other international organisations;
- the regulation of international trade;
- international development assistance.

The *observation and implementation* of various international obligations including the Human Rights Convention and obligations under EC law are not reserved. The Scottish Parliament is able, therefore, and in fact may be required, to legislate for the purpose of giving effect to international obligations as far as they relate to devolved matters. In the case of EC obligations, the Scottish Ministers may be liable under EC law to the same penalties as UK Ministers. Assisting UK Ministers is not reserved, and so Scottish Ministers are able to assist UK Ministers in the formulation, negotiation and implementation of policy relating to international obligations and are able to participate in European Council meetings and in meetings with our partners in the European Union.

3. The reservations relating to defence include:

- the defence of the realm;
- the army, navy and air forces and reserve forces;
- visiting forces international headquarters and defence organisations;
- trading with the enemy and enemy property.

Thus, all the matters for which the Ministry of Defence is responsible are covered by these reservations. Civil defence, however, is not reserved: in particular, plan-

---

[4] This did not prevent the Parliament discussing the question of the Protestant succession in December 1999, on a motion from the SNP group in the Parliament.

ning and organisation by civilian authorities, and the provision of non-combative defence against hostile attacks. There is also a specific exemption relating to sea fishing. The Royal Navy's Fishery Protection Squadron carries out various enforcement duties on behalf of the Fisheries Department (now DEFRA: Department for Environment Food and Rural Affairs) and Scottish Ministers are able to confer powers on members of the armed forces to enable this to continue.

4. The other matters included in the general reservations in Part I are:

- the registration and funding of political parties;
- the civil service;
- treason.

Specific Reservations Part II

Part II sets out specific, subject-related reservations by sections grouped under 11 heads. The heads are:

● *Head A – Financial and Economic Matters*

These include the issue and circulation of money, taxes and excise duties, government borrowing and lending, the exchange rate, the Bank of England and control over UK public expenditure. Specifically excepted are local taxes which partially fund local government expenditure, currently the council tax and non-domestic rates. The reservation of public expenditure does not affect the Scottish Parliament's ability to allocate its own resources. This section also reserves the currency, financial services (except fixing the dates of bank holidays), financial markets and money laundering.

● *Head B – Home Affairs*

This head covers a miscellany of matters dealt with by the Home Office including various aspects of the misuse of drugs: possession, production, supply, import and export, and trafficking. The Scottish Parliament, however, has powers in key areas such as education, health, social work, and criminal prosecution. Immigration, nationality, and extradition are reserved although certain executive powers of the Secretary of State are transferred to the Scottish Ministers. National security, official secrets, the interception of communication, and terrorism are reserved under this head as are firearms, data protection, and scientific procedures on live animals. Elections to the House of Commons, the European Parliament and the Scottish Parliament itself are reserved but the Scottish Parliament has power to legislate for all aspects of local government elections except for the franchise. The Parliament can, therefore, change the electoral system for local council elections, eg by the introduction of a form of proportional representation and, indeed, one of the first acts of the Scottish Executive after the May 1999 elections was to set up a working group with a remit, amongst other things, to advise on how a such a system could be introduced.[5] Following their findings, the coalition partnership deal between Labour

---

[5] The *Renewing Local Democracy Group*, chaired by Richard Kerley.

and the Liberal Democrats, formed after the 2003 elections, proposes to introduce the Single Transferable Vote system of Proportional Representation, for local council elections. Betting, gaming, lotteries, and various aspects of the classification of films and the distribution of video recordings are also reserved.

• *Head C – Trade and Industry*

This head covers a large number of areas including the creation, operation, regulation, and dissolution of business associations. The phrase 'business associations' covers companies, partnerships, building societies, and various other bodies. The intention of the reservation is to ensure a level playing field for business within the UK. Charities and certain public bodies are excepted from this reservation. The reasoning behind the latter exception is to enable the Scottish Parliament to create and regulate public bodies which are business associations for devolved areas such as health, education, sport, urban regeneration, and the environment – areas in which Scottish quangos such as the Scottish Sports Council (now Sport Scotland) already exist.

Import and export control are reserved to ensure a level playing field for UK business, but as agriculture, fisheries and food are devolved, the movement of food, animal, animal products, plants, animal feed, fertilisers, and pesticides is excepted from this reservation.

Insolvency, competition (except for certain practices in the Scottish legal profession), intellectual property, consumer protection (except in relation to food safety), product standards, safety, and liability (except in relation to agriculture, fisheries and food) are all reserved under this head. The regulation of sea fishing outside the Scottish zone except in relation to Scottish fishing boats is reserved, as are weights and measures, telecommunications and postal services.

• *Head D – Energy*

The generation, distribution and supply of electricity is reserved. Most aspects of oil and gas are reserved, including the ownership of, exploration for, and exploitation of, deposits of oil and natural gas. However, the manufacture of gas is not reserved nor are the powers to provide assistance for onshore activities in support of offshore activities. Coal, including its ownership and exploitation, deep and open-cast coal mining and subsidence are all reserved. The only exceptions to this reservation are certain environmental duties. Nuclear energy and instal-lations, including nuclear safety and liability for nuclear occurrences are all reserved. However, duties in relation to the keeping and use of radioactive material, the disposal or accumulation of radioactive waste and the regulation of non-nuclear activities at nuclear installations are excepted from reservation. Energy conservation is reserved but the Scottish Parliament is specifically allowed to legislate for, and in general promote, energy efficiency.

• *Head E – Transport*

In the case of road transport, various aspects of road traffic regulation and road safety are reserved including the licensing of drivers, driving instruction and the licensing and registration of vehicles. The prosecution and punishment of offenders for a range of road traffic offences is also reserved. However, the Scottish Parliament is able to legislate on the promotion of road safety by local authorities. Scottish Ministers and UK Government Ministers are given concurrent powers in relation to road safety information and training.

The provision and regulation of railway services and rail transport security are reserved as is (not surprisingly) the Channel Tunnel but the making of certain grants relating to railway services is excepted from reservation.

In the case of transport by sea, marine safety, navigation rights, the regulation of the British merchant fleet and all matters relating to the employment of seafarers are reserved. The Scottish Parliament, however, has the power to pass legislation relating to ports, harbours and piers. It also has the power to deal with the regulation of works which may endanger or obstruct navigation. An important exception from reservation is financial assistance to bulk freight shipping services between the Highlands and Islands and locations outside Scotland which are necessary for the social and economic well-being of these remote communities.

The regulation of aviation and air transport, including air safety and security, are reserved as are arrangements to compensate and repatriate passengers when an air transport operator becomes insolvent. Exceptions from reservation relate mainly to the provision of airports and various airport controls.

Miscellaneous reservations under this Head cover the transport of radioactive material, standards for public passenger transport for the disabled and the carriage of dangerous goods.

• Head F – Social Security

This head reserves social security schemes financed by central or local expenditure which provide benefits to individuals. Examples include National Insurance, the Social Fund, housing, and council tax benefits. Exceptions to this reservation include the provision in exceptional circumstances for payments to people in need and services such as home-help and residential nursing accommodation. Various provisions for the maintenance of children are also excepted although the subject matter of the Child Support Acts 1991 and 1995 in general is reserved. Occupational, personal and war pensions are all reserved but the SA 1998 contains specific provision for the payment of pensions to former members and staff of the Scottish Parliament.

• Head G – Regulation of the Professions

The professions reserved are architects, the health professions, and auditors. The health professions include doctors, dentists, opticians, pharmacists, nurses, midwives and many others including veterinary surgeons. The Scottish Parliament, however, has the power to legislate on the vocational training of doctors and dentists.

• Head H – Employment

Employment rights and duties and industrial relations are reserved. The exception to this is the setting of wages for Scottish agricultural workers which comes under the remit of the Scottish Agricultural Wages Board. This means that the Scottish Parliament cannot legislate for a Scottish minimum wage. Health and safety at work are reserved but public safety in devolved areas is not, thus allowing the Scottish Parliament to legislate on, for example, the safety of sports grounds. Job search and support are reserved but the duties which Scottish Enterprise and Highlands and Islands Enterprise have to assist people seeking work to obtain training are excepted. Careers services are also excepted.

(There is no Head I.)

• *Head J – Health and Medicine*

Abortion, xenotransplantation, embryology, surrogacy, and genetics are all reserved. The justification is that all of these raise major ethical issues and/or require expertise to be pooled at a UK level to allow them to be regulated satisfactorily. The Scottish Parliament will, however, be able to legislate on all other matters of sexual health. Medicines, medical supplies, and poisons are reserved as is the regulation of prices for medical supplies for the National Health Service in Scotland. Schemes for the distribution of welfare foods (milk and vitamins) are reserved.

• *Head K – Media and Culture*

All regulatory responsibilities relating to television and radio broadcasting are reserved although some executive functions relating to the funding of Gaelic broadcasting are transferred to the Scottish Executive. The justification for the reservation is that the regulatory framework is an important aspect of the single market in the UK and that the management of the airwaves and of competition in the independent television sector requires to be carried out on a UK basis.

The Public Lending Right Scheme which provides payments to authors whose books are borrowed from public libraries is reserved as is the scheme by which the government indemnifies lenders for the loss of or damage to works of art and other objects.

• *Head L – Miscellaneous*

The determination of the salaries of judges of the Court of Session, sheriffs, members of the Scottish Lands Tribunal, and the Chairman of the Scottish Land Court are reserved but payment of the salaries is not. Payment will be made out of the Scottish Consolidated Fund and will not require the prior approval of the Scottish Parliament. This is in line with UK practice and is one of the measures designed to protect the independence of the judiciary.

Most aspects of equal opportunity are reserved. Equal opportunity is defined as the prevention, elimination or regulation of discrimination between persons on the grounds of sex or marital status, on racial grounds, or on grounds of disability, age, sexual orientation, language or social origin, or of other personal attributes, including beliefs or opinions, such as religious beliefs or political opinions. Excepted from reservation is the encouragement of equal opportunity and the observance of equal opportunity requirements and the imposition of duties on Scottish public bodies and cross-border public authorities with a view to securing that their functions are carried out with due regard to the need to meet equal opportunity requirements.

Also under this head comes the control of nuclear, biological, chemical and any other weapons of mass destruction.

Timescales, time zones, and the determination of summer time are reserved along with the date of Easter and the calendar generally. Excepted are the dates of bank, public and local holidays.

The Ordnance Survey is reserved as is the regulation of activities in outer space.

General Provisions (Part III)

This part of Sch 5 safeguards from reservation Scottish public bodies with no reserved functions and those which have mixed functions, some reserved and some devolved. Local councils are a good example of the latter, having responsibility for devolved functions such as education, housing and social work and for some reserved functions such as the regulations of weights and measures and the administration of housing benefit. It also safeguards the giving of financial assistance to industry to promote or sustain economic development or employment. This part also reserves the constitution, assets, liabilities, funding, and receipts of all the bodies reserved by name in Part II and specifically the Commission for Racial Equality, the Equal Opportunities Commission and the National Disability Council.

Thus it can be seen that, although the UK Government decided to use the retaining model for the division of responsibilities between the Scottish and the UK Parliaments, the list of reserved powers is very detailed. The list may be modified from time to time by an Order in Council. The Scottish Parliament is, however, free to make laws in all areas which are not listed in Sch 5 or s 29, ie the devolved areas. Not only that, it has power to amend or repeal existing Acts of the UK Parliament which relate to devolved matters. In addition, it should also be noted that the Scottish Ministers also have extensive powers to take decisions in areas where the Parliament itself does not have legislative competence. These powers may arise from 'executive devolution', or from specific powers given to them in other Acts of the UK Parliament besides the SA 1998.[6] Although, strictly speaking, Scottish Ministers will not be accountable to the Scottish Parliament when exercising powers derived in such ways, as the Parliament has the undoubted power to debate even non-devolved matters, it can be expected that the actions of Scottish Ministers in the exercise of such powers will be scrutinised by the Parliament, and it would be hard to see how a Scottish Executive (or individual Minister) which used such powers against the wishes of a majority of the Parliament could survive in office.

DEVOLVED MATTERS

Broadly speaking, the devolved areas are as follows:

Health

- overall responsibility for the NHS in Scotland including terms and conditions of service; public and mental health; education and training of health professionals.

---

[6] See ch 6 for a discussion of executive devolution.

Education and training

- pre-five, primary and secondary school education; teacher supply, training and conditions of service; the functions of Her Majesty's Inspectorate of Schools;
- further and higher education policy and funding, the functions of the Scottish Higher Education Funding Council; student support;
- science and research funding in support of devolved matters;
- training policy; vocational qualifications; careers advice and guidance.

Local government, social work and housing

- local government finance and local taxes;
- social work including children's hearings and the voluntary sector;
- housing including the functions of Scottish Homes (now Communities Scotland);
- land-use planning; building control; area regeneration including the designation of enterprise zones.

Economic development and transport

- the functions of Scottish Enterprise, Highlands and Islands Enterprise and local enterprise companies;
- financial assistance to industry subject to UK guidelines; inward investment including the functions of Locate in Scotland;
- promotion of trade and exports;
- promotion of tourism including the functions of the Scottish Tourist Board (now known as Visit Scotland);
- passenger and road transport; the Scottish road network; road safety; bus policy and concessionary fares; taxis and mini-cabs; some rail grant powers; the Strathclyde Passenger Transport Authority and Executive;
- air and sea transport covering ports, harbours and piers; freight shipping and ferry services; Highlands and Islands Airports Ltd; planning and environmental issues relating to airports;
- inland waterways.

Law and home affairs

- criminal law and procedure except for statutory offences relating to reserved matters including drugs and firearms;
- civil law except in relation to reserved matters;
- judicial appointments;
- the criminal justice and prosecution system;
- civil and criminal courts; tribunals concerned with devolved matters and the Scottish Council on Tribunals; legal aid;
- parole, the release of life prisoners, and alleged miscarriages of justice;
- prisons, the Scottish Prison Service; the treatment of offenders;
- police and fire services; civil defence and emergency planning;
- liquor licensing;

- protection of animals (domestic, captive and wild); zoo licensing; the control of dangerous wild animals and game.

Environment

- environmental protection; air, land and water pollution, and the functions of the Scottish Environmental Protection Agency; water supplies and sewerage; sustainable development policies within a UK framework;
- the natural heritage, countryside issues, the functions of Scottish Natural Heritage;
- the built heritage, and the functions of Historic Scotland;
- flood prevention, coast protection, and the safety of reservoirs.

Agriculture, forestry and fishing

- domestic agriculture including crofting; animal and plant health and animal welfare within a UK framework; implementation of measures under the Common Agricultural Policy;
- food standards;
- forestry including the Forestry Commission;
- domestic fisheries including inshore sea, salmon and freshwater fisheries and aquaculture; implementation of measures under the Common Fisheries Policy.

Sport and the arts

- sport and the functions of the Scottish Sports Council (now known as Sports Scotland);
- the arts and the functions of the National Library, National Museums, and National Galleries of Scotland; the Scottish Museums Council, the Scottish Arts Council, Scottish Screen, and support for Gaelic.

Miscellaneous

- statistics, public registers and records including the responsibilities of the Keeper of the Records, the Keeper of the Registers and the Registrar General for Scotland.

THE POWER TO AMEND ACTS OF THE UK PARLIAMENT AND SCHEDULE 4

The Scottish Parliament has the power to amend or repeal Acts of the UK Parliament which relate to devolved matters. There are, however, limits placed on this power.[7] These are detailed in the SA 1998, Sch 4 which is entitled 'Enactments etc. protected from modification'.

---

[7] SA 1998, s 29(2).

The Scottish Parliament cannot modify arts 4 and 6 of the Acts of Union of 1706–07 so far as they relate to freedom of trade. Nor can it modify various sections of the European Communities Act 1972, the Act by means of which the UK joined the European Communities. The Human Rights Act 1998 which incorporates much of the European Convention on Human Rights is protected in its entirety from modification by the Scottish Parliament. The law on reserved matters cannot be modified by the Scottish Parliament and 'law' is defined as including not only Acts and subordinate legislation of the UK Parliament, but also any rule of law which is not contained in an enactment the subject matter of which is a reserved matter. This protects common law rules relating to reserved matters.

Significantly, the entire SA 1998, apart from a few provisions, is protected from amendment. Most of the exceptions are relatively minor, but they also include s 70, which deals with accounts and audit, and s 91, which deals with the investigation of complaints of maladministration.

3 ELECTIONS AND MEMBERS

INTRODUCTION

The Scotland Act 1998 (SA 1998) established the Scottish Parliament with 129 members elected by the form of proportional representation known as the additional member system[1]. This combines the relative majority system, commonly known as 'first past the post', involving single member constituencies, with an additional element which 'tops up' the political parties' representation from registered party lists by allocating regional seats on the basis of a second vote cast not for an individual but for a political party. It is also possible for individuals without any political affiliation to stand as candidates. Thus there are 'constituency members' and 'regional members'. The SA 1998 refers to them simply as 'members' but the term 'MSP' has become the normal way in which they are described and, in law, the status of constituency and regional members is the same.

THE NUMBER OF MSPs

At a general election to the Scottish Parliament, 73 constituency members and 53 regional members are elected, the latter divided equally among eight regions. The SA 1998 specifies that the Orkney Islands and the Shetland Islands are to form separate constituencies. (These two island groups are combined to form a single constituency for the purposes of elections to the House of Commons). The other constituencies for the Scottish Parliament are, at present, identical to the constituencies used for elections to the House of Commons. So there are 72 constituencies at Westminster and 73 in the Scottish Parliament.

However, the SA 1998 as originally enacted contained provisions which would have led to a reduction in the number of both constituency and regional MSPs. The reason for this is that the SA 1998 links the number of seats in the Scottish Parliament to the number of constituencies in the House of Commons and further requires the ratio of regional seats to the number of constituency seats to be 56 to 73, so far as is reasonably practicable[2]. Another provision of the SA 1998 requires the number of constituencies at Westminster to be reduced from the present 72[3]. The way the Act does this is as follows. The Parliamentary Constituencies Act 1986 (PCA 1986) contained, until 1998, a provision that the number of constituencies in Scotland should not be less than 71. This resulted in the average number of electors (the electoral quota) in Scottish constituencies being significantly lower than the average number of electors in an English constituency[4]. In

---

[1] See ss 1–18 of the SA 1998 for the provisions relating to MSPs and elections.

[2] SA 1998, Schedule.1.

[3] SA 1998, s 86.

[4] In 1997, Scotland had an average of 55,339 electors per constituency while England had an average of 69,578 electors per constituency.

other words, Scotland has more MPs per head of population than England. As a concession to the feeling that such relative over-representation at Westminster could no longer be justified once the Scottish Parliament had been established, the SA 1998 amended the PCA 1986 by removing that minimum of 71. In addition, the SA 1998 lays down that for the first review of parliamentary boundaries after the passing of the SA 1998, the electoral quota for England must be used to determine the appropriate number of Scottish seats at Westminster[5]. This would mean that the number of Scottish constituencies would fall to about 57 rather than the present 72.

The task of reviewing parliamentary constituency boundaries in Scotland is allocated to the Boundary Commission for Scotland and it is statutorily bound to conduct a general review between 8 and 12 years from the date of the report of its last general review. As its last report was submitted to the Secretary of State for Scotland in 1994, the Commission's next report must be made between 2002 and 2006. The Commission published its draft proposals in February 2002. As the Commission is able to take into account special geographical considerations which allow them to depart from the strict application of the electoral quota, its provisional recommendations provide for 59 constituencies for Scotland rather than 57.

As the SA 1998 ties the number of constituencies for the Scottish Parliament to the number of constituencies at Westminster (with special provision for the Orkney and Shetland Islands), the number of constituency MSPs would be reduced to 60, and as the ratio of regional seats to constituency seats should be, as far as practicable, the same as in the original arrangement, that is 56 to 73, the number of regional members would be reduced to around 44, between 5 or 6 per region. These provisions in the SA 1998 were extremely controversial. It was argued by many MSPs and by the Presiding Officer that the work of the Scottish Parliament would be undermined by a reduction in the number of members. During the passage of the Scotland Bill through the UK Parliament in 1998, however, government Ministers had made it clear that they would consider representations to amend the SA 1998 at some time in the future so as to remove the link between the number of Scottish constituencies in the House of Commons and the number of members of the Scottish Parliament. The Secretary of State for Scotland reiterated that view in September 2000 and, in 2001, a consultation exercise was launched to ascertain the views of the public. The overwhelming response was that, in the interests of stability, the Scottish Parliament should continue to operate with 129 MSPs. It was also argued that a reduction in the number of regional members would reduce the proportional element of the electoral system. On the other hand, some argued that difficulties would arise if the boundaries of the UK and Scottish parliamentary constituencies were not co-terminous.

In December 2002, the Secretary of State for Scotland announced in the House of Commons that, in the interests of the Scottish Parliament's stability, she would seek to have the SA 1998 amended. However, because of the concerns about the loss of co-terminosity, she proposed to set up an independent commission to examine the issues which might arise as a result of different constituency boundaries. This commission is to be established after the Scottish Parliament elections in 2007, and after the report of the Boundary Commission for Scotland

---

[5] SA 1998, s 86.

relating to the number of UK Parliamentary constituencies has been dealt with by the UK Parliament.

Thus the number of MSPs looks likely to remain at 129 for some time to come.

THE WEST LOTHIAN QUESTION

It should be said, however, that the way in which the SA 1998 sought to deal with the issue of Scottish representation at Westminster did not guarantee that such over-representation might not arise again in the future[6]. Furthermore, although the reduction in the number of MPs for Scottish constituencies at Westminster addresses one apparent anomaly produced by devolution in the constitutional arrangement of the UK as a whole, it does not meet the central issue raised by the 'West Lothian Question'[7], namely the question as to whether it is acceptable for the MPs for Scottish constituencies at Westminster to make laws for England on subjects on which they are unable to legislate for Scotland as such subjects now fall within the remit of the Scottish Parliament.[8] That question has led to increasing debate about the implications of devolution to Scotland and Wales for constitutional arrangements for England, in which numerous proposals have been put forward, including regional government for England, the establishment of an English Grand Committee and the setting up of a fully fledged parliament for England.[9]

CONSTITUENCY AND REGIONAL MEMBERS

In the single-member constituencies, the successful candidate is the one who receives the most votes on the straightforward 'first past the post' basis which currently applies in both local council and Westminster elections. Such constituency members are essentially elected as individuals although, in practice, most stand as the candidate of a political party. In the first general election to the Scottish Parliament, in May 1999, 72 of the 73 constituency members elected were candidates of political parties.[10] In the second general election in May 2003, 71 of the constituency members elected were candidates of political parties.[11]

Seven regional members are elected in each of eight Scottish regions. In the first general election, the boundaries of each region were the same as the 1996

---

[6] On this, see John Curtice, 'Reinventing the Yo-Yo? A Comment on the Electoral Provisions of the Scotland Bill' in Scottish Affairs, No 23, Spring 1998, p 41.

[7] Named after the Labour MP for West Lothian and later Linlithgow, Tam Dalyell, who frequently raised this issue after devolution for Scotland was proposed in the 1970s.

[8] This issue flared up again in 2003 when John Reid, the Scottish MP for Hamilton North and Bellshill, became the Secretary of State for Health, dealing with English health matters while having no responsibility for health matters in Scotland as these are devolved to the Scottish Parliament. It was also a matter of contention in the House of Commons that the votes of Scottish MPs preserved the government's majorities in relation to the abolition of foxhunting in England and the establishment of foundation hospitals in England

[9] See ch 12.

[10] In 1999, Dennis Canavan, the Labour MP for Falkirk West at Westminster, was deemed by his party to be 'not good enough' to stand for the Scottish Parliament as an official Labour candidate. He stood as an independent in Falkirk West and won the seat with 54.98% of the votes cast. He stood again as an independent in 2003, holding the seat this time with 55.69% of the votes cast.

[11] The two MSPs who did not stand as candidates of a political party were Dennis Canavan (see n 10 above) and Jean Turner who stood on the single issue of opposition to a local hospital closure.

boundaries for European Parliamentary constituencies. However, the choice of the European constituency as the basis for a region for the election of the regional members of the Scottish Parliament was purely a matter of administrative convenience; there is no link between the MSPs and the European constituency. Any link would have become superfluous with the abolition of constituencies for individual members of the European Parliament which took effect in 1999. If the number of regional members were to change as a result of a change in the number of constituencies, the boundaries of the regions would no longer have any connection with the former European parliamentary constituency boundaries.

In each region a registered political party[12] may submit a list of candidates for election as regional members. Each list may have up to 12 names on it (this allows for the filling of any vacancies which may arise from time to time). In addition, an individual without a party political affiliation may stand as an individual candidate for election as a regional member. The list system gives small political parties and individuals an enhanced opportunity to gain seats. The number of candidates on the lists rose from 500 in the 1999 election to 605 in 2003. A large number of parties put forward candidates, including the Green Party (which won seven seats), the Scottish Socialist Party (which won six seats) and the Scottish Senior Citizens Unity Party (which won one seat). Other parties which put forward lists of candidates (unsuccessfully) included, among many others, the Communist Party, the Monster Raving Loony Party, the Humanist Party, the Pro-Life Party and the Natural Law Party. In addition, a number of individuals stood as regional candidates on a single issue basis such as opposition to local hospital closures and the preservation of the Scottish fishing industry.

The SA 1998 permits a person to stand for election both as a constituency member (in only one constituency) and as a regional member provided that the constituency lies within the region concerned. The political parties used this as a fall-back mechanism in the first Scottish general election in 1999. Donald Dewar, the then leader of the Labour Party in Scotland, stood as the Labour candidate in the Anniesland constituency in Glasgow. He was also at the top of the Labour Party's regional list for Glasgow to ensure that he was elected to the Parliament even if defeated in the Anniesland constituency[13]. The leaders of the Scottish Conservative Party, the Scottish National Party, and the Scottish Socialist Party adopted the same belt and braces approach in both the 1999 and the 2003 elections[14]; the leader of the Green Party stood only as a regional member.

Although it is unlikely that anyone would be nominated by more than one political party or stand both as a party candidate and as an individual candidate, there are provisions in the SA 1998 to ensure that this is not possible[15].

---

[12] I e registered in terms of the Political Parties, Elections and Referendums Act 2000.

[13] The official party reason for putting the leader of the party at the top of the regional list, as well as having him stand as a constituency member, was to maximise the regional vote for the party by having a well-known name at the top of the party list.

[14] In 1999 the leaders of the Scottish Conservative Party and the Scottish Socialist Party failed to win constituency seats but were elected as regional members, while the leaders of the Labour Party and the Scottish National Party were elected as constituency members. In 2003 only the leader of the Scottish Socialist Party, Tommy Sheridan, failed to win a constituency seat and was elected as a regional member.

The leader of the Scottish Liberal Democrats, Jim Wallace, did not appear to have the same doubts as to his ability to win a constituency seat. His confidence was justified as he won 67.39% of the votes cast in the Orkney constituency, the highest personal vote of any candidate in the 1999 election. In 2003 his share of the votes fell to 45.71%, but he was elected again as the constituency member.

[15] SA 1998, s 5(7) and (8).

At a general election for the Scottish Parliament, each voter has two votes. One vote is cast to choose a named candidate from those standing in that voter's constituency to be the constituency member. The other vote is cast to elect regional members. It may be cast either for the list submitted in that region by a registered political party or for an individual who is standing for election as a regional member. The voter, however, cannot choose to vote for a particular candidate on a party list; if he or she wishes to vote for the party list, he or she must do so *en bloc*. This type of list is known as a 'closed' list.

In an attempt to avoid confusion, the ballot papers for the constituency seats are a different colour from the ballot papers for the regional seats. In 1999, the ballot papers were lilac and peach, respectively; in 2003 they were aquamarine and peach. The local council elections are held on the same day as the elections to the Scottish Parliament and the ballot papers for these elections are white.

THE ALLOCATION OF SEATS

The votes cast for the constituency candidates are counted first and the candidate who secures the majority of votes in each constituency is declared to be the MSP for that constituency. The reason that the constituency seats are decided first is because the regional member seats are allocated on the basis of correcting imbalances brought about by the 'first past the post' system used in the constituency seats. If a party secures fewer constituency seats than its overall electoral support would suggest, it is allocated more of the regional seats to bring about a result in which the total number of seats won by any party is more proportional to the total number of votes cast for it in each region.

The calculation of the regional figures and the allocation of the regional seats is somewhat complex and the reader should refer to Table 3.2 at the end of the chapter for an example of the calculation. For each political party which has submitted a list of candidates, the total number of regional votes cast throughout the region is divided by the number of constituency seats won by that party plus one. The resulting figure is called the 'regional figure'. Parties which did not gain any constituency seats are also involved in this calculation. Each time a party gains a regional member seat, that party's regional figure is recalculated. The regional figure for individual candidates is the total number of votes cast for the individual in all the constituencies included in the region.

The first regional member seat is allocated to the party or individual with the highest regional figure. This will not necessarily be the party with the highest total of regional votes as account is taken of the number of constituency seats already won by the parties. The second and subsequent seats are then allocated on the basis of the recalculated regional figures. Seats are allocated to the persons on a party's list in the order in which they appear on the list, disregarding, of course, anyone who has already won a constituency seat.

In calculating the allocation of regional seats, account is taken only of the number of votes cast for the regional lists. A party which received a total of votes in the election of constituency members which varied substantially from the total of the votes cast for their regional list would not have that difference taken into account in the allocation of the additional seats from the regional list.

The system for allocating seats does in broad terms result in an allocation of seats in proportion to the number of votes cast for the candidates on the regional lists. It does not, however, result in complete proportionality as can be seen from Table 3.1 below.

Political party	% of FPTP votes	% of FPTP seats	% of regional votes	% of regional seats
Labour	35%	63%	29%	7%
SNP	24%	12%	21%	32%
Conservatives	17%	4%	16%	27%
Liberal Democrats	15%	18%	12%	7%
Scottish Socialist Party	6%	0%	7%	11%
Green Party	Did not contest	N/A	7%	12.5%

Table 3.1   2003 election figures

It should be noted that an automatic side-effect of any reduction in the number of regional members elected to the Parliament is that the proportionality of the final result will be reduced. The reason for this is that a reduced number of seats means that if one party gets more than its fair share of constituency seats there will be fewer regional seats available to correct that imbalance.

ELECTIONS AND BY-ELECTIONS

Ordinary and extraordinary general elections

Members of the Scottish Parliament elected from both constituencies and regional lists are normally elected at the same time in a Scotland-wide general election. The first of these was held on 6 May 1999 and the second on 1 May 2003. The term of office of an MSP begins on the day on which the member is declared to be returned and ends with the dissolution of the Parliament. Subsequent ordinary general elections take place on the first Thursday in May four years after the previous general election, with some flexibility being provided in that an ordinary general election can be held within a period running from one month before until one month after the first Thursday in May.

Extraordinary general elections can take place earlier than four years after the previous election in two situations. The first situation in which an extraordinary general election must be held is where a majority of MSPs amounting to not less than two-thirds of the total number of members of the Parliament vote for an earlier election. The second set of circumstances is where, for some reason or other, the office of First Minister has been vacant for a period of (normally) 28 days.

The first situation would arise only if a clear majority of the political parties represented in the Parliament wanted to hold an earlier general election because, for example, government had become unworkable due to a breakdown of a coalition. A two-thirds majority would probably require the support of three of the major political party groups. The requirement for such a majority thus makes it impossible for a government with a small majority to call an early general election at a time which it considers might suit its party political interests. This is in contrast to the situation in the UK Parliament which does not have a fixed term and the Prime Minister can call a general election at a time which suits him or her.

In the second situation, the office of First Minister could be vacant for a variety of reasons. It could be that, after an ordinary general election, the MSPs fail to agree on a nomination for the post of First Minister because of a simple majority of MSPs voting against every nominee – if 28 days elapse without a resolution of this impasse an extraordinary general election would have to be held. If, after an extraordinary general election held as a result of such a failure to agree on a nomination, there continued thereafter to be no agreement on the nomination of a First Minister, theoretically further extraordinary elections could continue to be held. In practice, however, this situation is very unlikely to arise as the political parties responsible for repeated elections would fear a backlash from the electorate.

The office of First Minister might become vacant as a result of the death of the incumbent. This happened in October 2000 when Donald Dewar, the first First Minister, died unexpectedly. The statutory 28-day period for filling the post caused the Labour Party some difficulty on this occasion. The period starts to run from the day on which the death occurred. Decency demanded that there should be a period of mourning and that campaigning by contenders to fill the vacancy should not begin at least until the funeral was over. This cut the period to about 21 days. The Labour Party's internal procedures for electing a party leader in Scotland from among the Labour MSPs (who would become the new First Minister) take a much longer time than that. In the event, Donald Dewar's successor, Henry McLeish, was elected by an electoral college consisting of all Labour MSPs and the Scottish Labour Party's Executive Committee ten days after Mr Dewar's death. Mr McLeish was duly nominated as First Minister by the Scottish Parliament five days later and was formally appointed to the post by the Queen on the following day. His formal endorsement as Leader of the Scottish Labour Party took place about six weeks later.

Another possibility is that the office of First Minister might become vacant as a result of the incumbent tendering his resignation. This happened in 2001 when Henry McLeish had been First Minister for just over a year. As a result of press inquiries into various lets of his constituency offices and the resulting pressure from opposition parties in the Parliament, Mr McLeish tendered his resignation in November 2001. Although there was no need for the delay necessary after a death, the 28-day period was again too short for the Scottish Labour Party to carry out its full procedures for the election of a new party leader and, to avoid the requirement of an extraordinary election, Jack McConnell was elected by the same truncated procedure described above, nominated by the Parliament, appointed by the Queen within the 28 days and formally endorsed as party leader by the members of the Scottish Labour Party some weeks later.

A further possibility, and one which has not yet occurred, is that the First Minister ceases to be an MSP (otherwise than as a result of the Parliament being dissolved for an election). This might happen by the First Minister simply deciding to resign from the Parliament altogether or by the First Minister being disqualified for some reason. Reasons for disqualification include bankruptcy, mental illness and being convicted of an offence and sentenced to a term of imprisonment of more than a year. Again, the vacancy must be filled within 28 days or an extraordinary general election will be triggered.

By-elections

In the case of a seat falling vacant between elections, different mechanisms apply depending on whether the seat was previously held by a constituency member or a regional member. If the seat of a constituency member falls vacant for any reason such as death or resignation, a by-election in the constituency will be held, normally within three months, to elect a replacement. However, if the latest date for holding the by-election would bring it within three months of the next ordinary election to the Parliament, the vacancy will remain unfilled until the next general election. This is to avoid the expense of the election process for the sake of filling the seat for only a few months.

If the seat of a regional member falls vacant, different procedures apply depending on whether the seat was previously held by a member elected from a party list or a member who had been elected as an individual member. In the former case, the vacancy is filled by the next person on that party's list who is willing to serve and who is acceptable to the party concerned[16]. In the latter case, the vacancy remains unfilled until the next general election.

The first by-election was brought about by the resignation, for family reasons, in December 1999, of the constituency member for Ayr. The by-election was held in March 2000 and was won by the Conservative candidate, thus giving the Conservatives their first constituency seat. This had no effect on the allocation of regional seats which remained fixed until the general election of 2003.

Miscellaneous matters

The right to vote in elections to the Scottish Parliament is based on similar principles to the right to vote in elections to the UK Parliament. However, it is extended to those who are entitled to vote in local government elections. The effect of this is to extend the right to vote to members of the House of Lords and to citizens of the member states of the European Union who are resident in Scotland[17].

The rules relating to disqualification from membership of the Scottish Parliament are similar to those for the House of Commons and are set out in ss 15 and 16 of the SA 1998. Thus judges, civil servants (including the staff of the Scottish Executive and its agencies), members of the armed forces, members of police forces, and members of foreign legislatures are disqualified. Holders of certain public offices – for example, members of Scottish Enterprise, the Scottish Environmental Protection Agency, the Scottish Qualifications Authority and the Crofters Commission – are also disqualified. However, members of the House of Lords (apart from the Law Lords) who are disqualified from membership of the House of Commons are not ineligible to be MSPs merely because of their membership of the House of Lords. Three members of the House of Lords were elected as MSPs in the first general election in 1999 and two in 2003[18].

Aliens are also disqualified. An alien is a person who is not a British citizen, a Commonwealth citizen, a citizen of the Irish Republic or a citizen of the European Union. A citizen of the European Union must, however, be resident in the UK to be eligible to stand. Persons under the age of 21 are disqualified as are undischarged bankrupts, persons suffering from mental illness, convicted prisoners serving a sentence of more than one year and persons guilty of corrupt or illegal

---

[16] SA 1998, s 10(4)–(5A). This amendment was made to the Act when it was realised, belatedly, that a person on a party's list may have changed parties.

[17] The fact that citizens of the European Union resident in Scotland were entitled to vote was misunderstood by some polling clerks in the first general election to the Scottish Parliament in 1999. As a result several EU citizens were denied the vote to which they were entitled.

[18] Lord Steel (Liberal Democrat), Lord Watson (Labour), and Lord James Douglas-Hamilton (Conservative) in 1999 and Lord Watson and Lord James Douglas-Hamilton in 2003.

election practices. Senior local government officers who hold what are called 'politically restricted posts' are also ineligible to stand.

Persons who have been ordained or who are ministers of religion of any denomination, many of whom were, until 2001[19], disqualified from standing for election to the House of Commons, are eligible to stand for election to the Scottish Parliament.

The date for the first general election on 6 May 1999 was set by the Secretary of State for Scotland and he or she continues to have the power to make rules for the conduct of elections, including rules on the procedure for electoral registration and on election expenses for both candidates and political parties[20]. This power is exercised by the use of secondary legislation, which in this particular case requires the approval of both Houses of the Westminster Parliament[21].

The Labour and Liberal Democrat representatives on the Scottish Constitutional Convention[22] came to an informal agreement that in the first election to the Parliament in 1999 they would attempt to field an equal number of male and female candidates in winnable seats. Although some wanted this to be put into the SA 1998, this was not done on the ground that it might fall foul of anti-sex discrimination legislation in force at that time[23]. In their procedures for the selection of candidates for the constituency seats, the Labour Party 'twinned' pairs of constituencies in most of Scotland and instructed their members to select one man and one woman candidate for each pair. There was no challenge to this from within the Labour Party. However, despite the agreement, the Liberal Democrats did not adopt such an approach as they were unable to get the party's agreement to the proposal.

The Labour Party's procedures resulted in 28 men and 28 women being elected as Labour MSPs in the first general election in 1999. Of the Liberal Democrat MSPs elected in that election, 15 were men and only 2 were women. The comparable figures for the SNP were 20 men and 15 women, and for the Conservatives, 15 men and 3 women. For the second general election, in 2003, most of the sitting MSPs were re-adopted as candidates and thus there was no requirement for any artificial procedures on the part of the Labour Party. That election resulted in 78 men and 51 women being elected: at 35.9% this is one of the highest percentages of female representation in parliaments throughout the world. Only the Welsh Assembly and the Swedish parliament have a higher proportion. The breakdown by party is: Labour – 28 women and 22 men; SNP – 9 women and 18 men; Conservatives – 4 women and 14 men; Liberal Democrats – 2 women and 15 men; Scottish Socialists – 4 women and 2 men; Independents –

---

[19] The prohibition on persons who had been ordained standing for election to the House of Commons was removed by the House of Commons (Removal of Clergy Disqualification) Act 2001. This change in the law was hastened by the Labour Party in Greenock and Inverclyde selecting a person who had been ordained as a Roman Catholic Priest as their candidate for the UK Parliamentary election in 2001.

[20] The office of Secretary of State for Scotland ceased to function as a full-time post in June 2003; see ch 7.

[21] SA 1998, s 12 and Sch 7.

[22] For the Scottish Constitutional Convention, see ch 1.

[23] Prior to the 1997 general election, the Labour Party had attempted to increase the number of women MPs at Westminster by having all-women shortlists. This was successfully challenged before an industrial tribunal by two male aspiring candidates. See *Jepson and Dyas-Elliot v The Labour Party* [1996] IRLR 116. In response to this the UK Parliament passed the Sex Discrimination (Election Candidates) Act 2002, which amends the Sex Discrimination Act 1975, and makes all-women shortlists lawful for any parliamentary and local government election.

2 men and 2 women. In neither of the two general elections held so far has a member of any of the ethnic minority communities in Scotland been elected. The additional member system could ensure the election of ethnic minority candidates if the political parties put them at the top of their lists.

Dual mandates

Dual mandate is the term given to a situation where an individual is an elected member of two bodies and therefore has a mandate from two sets of electors. The SA 1998 does not prohibit dual mandates and thus it is possible for someone who is an MP in the UK Parliament, a Member of the European Parliament or a councillor to be elected as a member of the Scottish Parliament. In the first election to the Parliament in 1999, fifteen serving MPs, one MEP and three councillors were elected and did not resign their seats at Westminster, in Europe or in their local councils[24]. In the 2003 election, it would appear that only one person, a councillor, has a dual mandate. There are, however, provisions which prevent an MSP who is also an MP or an MEP from drawing two full salaries[25], and a person who holds ministerial office in the UK Government is not permitted to be a member of the Scottish Executive[26]. Westminster MPs, such as Donald Dewar and Henry McLeish, who held office in the UK Government as Ministers in the Scottish Office at the time of the first election in 1999, resigned from these posts on election to the Scottish Parliament. The political parties came to an informal agreement that there would be no dual mandate members after the UK general election of 2001. As a result, at that election all but one of those members who held dual mandates in the Scottish and UK Parliaments opted not to stand again for the UK Parliament. The other, Alex Salmond of the SNP, opted to stand for election to the UK Parliament and resigned his seat in the Scottish Parliament.

THE RIGHTS AND OBLIGATIONS OF MSPs

The Register of Interests and the Code of Conduct

Members of the Scottish Parliament have certain obligations imposed on them to ensure that they do not act in an improper manner. They and their staff are subject to the Prevention of Corruption Acts 1889 to 1916 which impose penalties for the corrupt making or acceptance of payments in money or in kind for activity in connection with the business of the Parliament[27].

The SA 1998 also requires the Parliament to establish a register of members' interests, open to inspection by the public[28]. The initial rules relating to the register were made for the first MSPs by a transitional order made by the Secretary of State for Scotland in May 1999. The requirements of the transitional order are temporary and the registration of MSPs' interests will, in time, be governed by an

---

[24] Those members of the Scottish Parliament (especially those who were members of the Scottish Executive) who were also members of the UK Parliament found it difficult to attend meetings at Westminster and received some criticism from opposition parties for poor attendance at the time.

[25] See p 31 for salaries.

[26] SA 1998, s 44.

[27] SA 1998, s 43.

[28] SA 1998, s 39.

Act of the Scottish Parliament. All MSPs and the Lord Advocate and the Solicitor General for Scotland are required to register certain financial interests, including benefits in kind, and must declare any interest before taking part in proceedings of the Parliament which relate to that interest. The registrable interests include: remuneration, other than the salaries and expenses paid to MSPs; unremunerated directorships; certain donations to election expenses; sponsorship; overseas visits; certain gifts, interests in heritable property and shareholdings.

The Standing Orders of the Parliament require it to set up a number of committees which are called mandatory committees[29]. One of these is the Standards Committee and this committee must be established within 21 sitting days of a general election. The remit of the Standards Committee is to consider and report on the adoption, amendment and application of a code of conduct for MSPs and on whether the conduct of individual MSPs is in accordance with Standing Orders and with the code of conduct. The Standards Committee spent several months in the early days of the first Parliament in the drafting of a detailed code of conduct.

The rules relating to the registration and declaration of interests have been embodied in the Code of Conduct for Members of the Scottish Parliament. The terms of the code were agreed by the Parliament in February 2000 and came into force immediately.

The SA 1998 also contains provisions relating to paid advocacy. The code sets down detailed rules relating to paid advocacy which is defined as advocating any cause for any form of payment or benefit in kind, including hospitality[30]. Members of the Scottish Parliament who receive remuneration (other than their salaries and expenses as MSPs) are also prohibited from encouraging other MSPs to act on their behalf in an attempt to get around the rules against paid advocacy.

Also included in the code of conduct are rules relating to contacts with lobbyists, the regulation of cross-party groups, general conduct and conduct in the chamber and committees of the Parliament. One of the first tasks of the Standards Committee was to investigate claims made in a Sunday newspaper that a firm of lobbyists could guarantee access to Scottish Ministers. This became known as the 'Lobbygate' affair. After interviewing various Ministers, their staff and members of the firm of lobbyists concerned, the members of the Standards Committee concluded that there was no truth in the allegations but an early priority for the committee became the regulation of the lobbying of MSPs.

The Parliament established a Parliamentary Standards Commissioner in 2002 to investigate allegations of breaches of the code of conduct by MSPs[31]. Any complaint about the conduct of an MSP should be made in writing and sent to the

---

[29] For the committees of the Parliament generally, see pp 39–45.

[30] For an interesting example of a legal challenge to an MSP, alleging breach of the advocacy rule and acceptance of benefits in kind, see *Whaley and Others v Lord Watson and the Scottish Parliamentary Corporate Body* 2000 SLT 475. Lord Watson MSP introduced a member's Bill (the Protection of Wild Mammals Bill) the purpose of which was to ban foxhunting by dogs. He received legal and administrative assistance, including advice on drafting the Bill, from the Scottish Campaign against Hunting with Dogs which the supporters of foxhunting considered to be benefits in kind.

The Inner House of the Court of Session decided that it had no power to prevent MSPs from breaching the members' interests rules. The rules can only be enforced by retrospective sanctions which include a fine.

[31] Scottish Parliamentary Standards Commissioner Act 2002.

Scottish Parliamentary Standards Commissioner who will investigate the complaint, if it is admissible, and report to the Standards Committee. After the Standards Committee has considered the Standards Commissioner's report, it in turn reports to the Parliament. If the Standards Committee has recommended the imposition of sanctions against the Member, a decision on sanctions is made by the Parliament. Sanctions include restricting a Member from participating in certain proceedings of the Parliament, excluding a Member from all proceedings of the Parliament, the removal of all or part of the Member's allowances and the withdrawal of various rights and privileges. Certain breaches of the code in relation to the registration and declaration of interests and the paid advocacy rule may be criminal offences and a Member found guilty is liable on summary conviction to a fine not exceeding level 5 on the standard scale.

Members of the Scottish Parliament are protected by what is called 'absolute privilege' against any person seeking to take action against them on account of any statement made by them in proceedings of the Parliament. The publication of any statement made under the authority of the Parliament is similarly absolutely privileged[32]. As a result, MSPs cannot be made to pay damages if such a statement is defamatory, even if the statement is made maliciously. The justification for this is that it is in the public interest for MSPs to be able to debate and discuss matters freely without any fear of being sued. This freedom of speech is somewhat similar to the freedom of speech enjoyed by MPs at Westminster. Unlike proceedings at Westminster, however, the proceedings of the Scottish Parliament are subject to the law of contempt of court, except in respect of publications made in proceedings of the Parliament in relation to a Bill or subordinate legislation, or to the extent that a publication consists of a fair and accurate report of such proceedings made in good faith[33]. The Parliament's Standing Orders provide for a 'sub judice' rule. This means that an MSP must not, in the proceedings of the Parliament, refer to any matter in relation to which legal proceedings are active, except to the extent permitted by the Presiding Officer; and if an MSP does refer to such a matter, the Presiding Officer may order that member not to do so[34]. However, nothing in this rule is to prevent the Parliament from legislating on any matter.

It should be noted that in any legal proceedings against the Parliament, a court may not make an order for interdict (or similar order) against the Parliament, but may make a declarator of the legal position instead[35]. The purpose of this is to afford the Parliament a measure of protection against attempts to interfere with its business through the use of legal proceedings. It is not yet clear what the consequences are for the Parliament of a declaratory order from a court.

Similarly, a court may not make an order for interdict (or similar order) against any MSP, the Presiding Officer or his deputies, or any member of staff of the Parliament in the Parliamentary corporation if the effect would be to give relief against the Parliament which could not have been given in proceedings against the Parliament. This provision is designed to prevent attempts to interfere with the business of the Parliament 'by the back door'. However, as a result of a decision of the Court of Session early in 2000, it is, clear that, in certain

---

[32] SA 1998, s 41.
[33] SA 1998, s 42.
[34] Scottish Parliament's Standing Orders, r 7.5.
[35] SA 1998, s 40(3), (4).

circumstances, it is possible for a court to grant an interdict against an individual MSP[36].

SALARIES

The Parliament is able to pay MSPs' salaries, allowances and pensions[37] and the basic salary of each MSP, regardless of whether the member was elected as a constituency or a regional member, was set in the first year of the Parliament's existence at £40,092. By 2003–4 that amount had risen to £49,315. The Scottish Parliament Salaries Scheme provides for an annual review of MSPs' salaries from April 2003 to maintain their salaries at 87.5% of the salary payable to Members of the House of Commons. Ministers receive an additional amount, depending on the level of seniority. The First Minister, for example, receives a ministerial allowance of £71,433 plus the basic salary of £49,315, giving him a total of £120,748[38]. If an MSP is also a member of the Westminster Parliament or of the European Parliament, he or she is entitled to receive the appropriate salary as well, but the Scottish Parliament must ensure that the element of salary which derives from membership of the Scottish Parliament is reduced[39]. The Parliament decided that the amount of the reduction should be two-thirds of the MSP's basic salary of £49,315. There is no reduction for MSPs who are also local authority councillors.

Members of the Scottish Parliament also receive a Members' Support Allowance of up to £50,700 per annum to enable the MSP to take on staff to assist the Member in carrying out parliamentary duties, establish and run an office in his or her constituency or region and meet with constituents. There are various other allowances, such as travel allowances and Edinburgh accommodation allowances. There is also a 'winding up allowance' for Members who cease to be MSPs.

The leaders of opposition parties which have at least 15 MSPs, none of whom hold ministerial office, are entitled to an allowance to take account of their responsibilities as party leaders. In addition, political party groups within the Parliament are entitled to financial assistance to enable them to perform their parliamentary duties. To be eligible for this, the party must have no more than one-fifth of their MSPs appointed as Members of the Scottish Executive or Junior Ministers.

After every election each MSP is required to take the oath of allegiance to the Crown within a specified period (normally two months). Until the oath is taken, he or she cannot participate in the proceedings of the Parliament, or receive any payment of salary or allowances. If the oath is not taken within the specified period, the MSP concerned automatically loses his or her seat in the Parliament[40]. This provision concentrated the minds of various MSPs of a republican bent in both 1999 and 2003. They all took the oath of allegiance, albeit under protest.

---

[36] *Whaley and Others v Lord Watson and the Scottish Parliamentary Corporate Body* 2000 SLT 475.
[37] SA 1998, s 81.
[38] As a result of his dual mandate, the first First Minister, Donald Dewar, was entitled to earn more per annum than the Prime Minister of the UK. He elected to forgo his entitlement to one-third of an MSP's salary.
[39] SA 1998, s 82.
[40] SA 1998, ss 83, 84.

TABLE 3.2

Allocating seats on the regional list

1. In each region, the number of votes cast for each party in the 'second vote' for a regional list is totalled.
2. This total is then divided by the figure which equals one plus the number of constituency members elected for that party in that region.
3. The first regional seat is then allocated to the political party, or a candidate standing as an individual, having the highest figure after the calculation in step 2 above has been carried out.
4. The total votes cast for each party in the region are then divided by the figure which equals one plus the number of constituency and regional members elected for that party in that region. Where the calculation results in a number which is not a whole number, that number may be rounded down to the nearest whole number by the exercise of the returning officer's discretion.
5. The next regional seat is then allocated to the political party, or candidate standing as an individual, now having the highest figure after the calculation in step 4 above has been carried out.
6. This process of recalculation of the figure for each party is then carried out until all seven places for regional members have been allocated.
7. Seats on the regional list are allocated to candidates in the order in which the political parties have placed them on the list prior to the election.

The following example shows how the system of allocation of seats was carried out in Glasgow. There are ten constituency seats and seven regional seats in Glasgow.

1. The number of individual constituency members elected was as follows:

Scottish Conservative and Unionist Party	0
Scottish Labour Party	10
Scottish Liberal Democrats	0
Scottish National Party	0
Scottish Socialist Party	0
Others	0

2. The number of regional list votes cast was as follows:

British National Party	2,344
Communist Party Peace Democracy Socialism	345
Pro Life Party	2,477
Scottish Conservative and Unionist Party	15,299
Scottish Green Party	14,570
Scottish Labour Party	77,040
Scottish Liberal Democrats	14,839
Scottish National Party	34,894
The Scottish People's Alliance	612

The Scottish Senior Citizens Unity Party	4,750
Scottish Socialist Party	31,116
Scottish Unionist Party	2,349
Socialist Labour Party	3,091
United Kingdom Independent Party	552

3. **The first seat**   The above totals were then divided by the figure of one plus the number of constituency members elected for each party to give the regional figure for each. As the Scottish Labour Party was the only party to win any seats, its figure of 77,040 is divided by 11 (10 + 1). The other parties' figures are divided by 1 (0 + 1) and therefore their regional figures are the same as in the table above. Calculated figures are rounded down to the nearest whole number. The winning party is marked*:

British National Party	2,344
Communist Party Peace Democracy Socialism	345
Pro Life Party	2,477
Scottish Conservative and Unionist Party	15,299
Scottish Green Party	14,570
Scottish Labour Party	7,003
Scottish Liberal Democrats	14,839
Scottish National Party	34,894*
The Scottish People's Alliance	612
The Scottish Senior Citizens Unity Party	4,750
Scottish Socialist Party	31,116
Scottish Unionist Party	2,349
Socialist Labour Party	3,091
United Kingdom Independent Party	552

As a result of this calculation, the SNP had the highest regional figure so the top person on its regional list was elected. Thus, the total number of MSPs elected for each party at that stage was as follows:

Scottish Labour Party	10
Scottish National Party	1
Others	0

4. **The second seat**   Since the SNP had won the first seat, its regional figure was recalculated by dividing its original regional figure by 2 (1 + 1), giving the following:

British National Party	2,344	
Communist Party Peace Democracy Socialism	345	
Pro Life Party	2,477	
Scottish Conservative and Unionist Party	15,299	
Scottish Green Party	14,570	
Scottish Labour Party	7,003	
Scottish Liberal Democrats	14,839	
Scottish National Party	17,447	(i e 34,894 ÷ 2)

The Scottish People's Alliance	612
The Scottish Senior Citizens Unity Party	4,750
Scottish Socialist Party	31,116*
Scottish Unionist Party	2,349
Socialist Labour Party	3,091
United Kingdom Independent Party	552

As a result of this calculation the party which now had the highest regional figure was the Scottish Socialist Party and so the person at the top of its list was elected. Thus, the total number of MSPs elected for each party at that stage was as follows:

Scottish Labour Party	10
Scottish National Party	1
Scottish Socialist Party	1
Others	0

5. **The third seat**   This time the regional figure for the Scottish Socialist Party was recalculated by being divided by 2 (1 + 1), giving the following figures:

British National Party	2,344	
Communist Party Peace Democracy Socialism	345	
Pro Life Party	2,477	
Scottish Conservative and Unionist Party	15,299	
Scottish Green Party	14,570	
Scottish Labour Party	7,003	
Scottish Liberal Democrats	14,839	
Scottish National Party	17,447*	
The Scottish People's Alliance	612	
The Scottish Senior Citizens Unity Party	4,750	
Scottish Socialist Party	15,558	(i e 31,116 ÷ 2)
Scottish Unionist Party	2,349	
Socialist Labour Party	3,091	
United Kingdom Independent Party	552	

The party which now had the highest figure was the Scottish Nationalist Party, which had won the first seat, therefore the second person on its list was elected. The number of seats for the parties were then as follows:

Scottish Labour Party	10
Scottish National Party	2
Scottish Socialist Party	1
Others	0

6. **The fourth seat**   The SNP's regional figure was recalculated. This time the SNP's original regional figure was divided by 3 (2 + 1). The following figures resulted:

| British National Party | 2,344 |
| Communist Party Peace Democracy Socialism | 345 |

Pro Life Party	2,477	
Scottish Conservative and Unionist Party	15,299	
Scottish Green Party	14,570	
Scottish Labour Party	7,003	
Scottish Liberal Democrats	14,839	
Scottish National Party	11,631	(i e 34,894 ÷ 3)
The Scottish People's Alliance	612	
The Scottish Senior Citizens Unity Party	4,750	
Scottish Socialist Party	15,558*	
Scottish Unionist Party	2,349	
Socialist Labour Party	3,091	
United Kingdom Independent Party	552	

The party which now had the highest figure was the Scottish Socialist Party, which had won the second seat, therefore the second person on its list was elected. The number of seats for the parties were then as follows:

Scottish Labour Party	10
Scottish National Party	2
Scottish Socialist Party	2
Others	0

7. **The fifth seat**   The Scottish Socialist Party's regional figure was recalculated. This time the SSP's original regional figure was divided by 3 (2 + 1). The following figures resulted:

British National Party	2,344	
Communist Party Peace Democracy Socialism	345	
Pro Life Party	2,477	
Scottish Conservative and Unionist Party	15,299*	
Scottish Green Party	14,570	
Scottish Labour Party	7,003	
Scottish Liberal Democrats	14,839	
Scottish National Party	11,631	
The Scottish People's Alliance	612	
The Scottish Senior Citizens Unity Party	4,750	
Scottish Socialist Party	10,372	(i e 31,116 ÷ 3)
Scottish Unionist Party	2,349	
Socialist Labour Party	3,091	
United Kingdom Independent Party	552	

The party which now had the highest figure was the Scottish Conservative and Unionist Party and therefore the person at the top of its list was elected. The numbers of seats for the parties were then as follows:

Scottish Labour Party	10
Scottish National Party	2
Scottish Socialist Party	2
Scottish Conservative and Unionist Party	1
Others	0

8. **The sixth seat** This time the regional figure for the Scottish Conservative and Unionist Party was recalculated by being divided by 2 (1+1). This resulted in the following figures:

British National Party	2,344	
Communist Party Peace Democracy Socialism	345	
Pro Life Party	2,477	
Scottish Conservative and Unionist Party	7,649	(ie 15,299 ÷ 2)
Scottish Green Party	14,570	
Scottish Labour Party	7,003	
Scottish Liberal Democrats	14,839*	
Scottish National Party	11,631	
The Scottish People's Alliance	612	
The Scottish Senior Citizens Unity Party	4,750	
Scottish Socialist Party	10,372	
Scottish Unionist Party	2,349	
Socialist Labour Party	3,091	
United Kingdom Independent Party	552	

The party with the highest figure was the Scottish Liberal Democrats and so the person at the top of its list was elected. The seats for the parties were thus:

Scottish Labour Party	10
Scottish National Party	2
Scottish Socialist Party	2
Scottish Conservative and Unionist Party	1
Scottish Liberal Democrats	1
Others	0

9. **The seventh seat** The last recalculation was carried out. The Scottish Liberal Democrats' regional figure was divided by 2 (1+1). The figures are as follows:

British National Party	2,344	
Communist Party Peace Democracy Socialism	345	
Pro Life Party	2,477	
Scottish Conservative and Unionist Party	7,649	
Scottish Green Party	14,570*	
Scottish Labour Party	7,003	
Scottish Liberal Democrats	7,419	(ie 14,839 ÷ 2)
Scottish National Party	11,631	
The Scottish People's Alliance	612	
The Scottish Senior Citizens Unity Party	4,750	
Scottish Socialist Party	10,372	
Scottish Unionist Party	2,349	
Socialist Labour Party	3,091	
United Kingdom Independent Party	552	

The party with the highest regional figure was the Scottish Green Party, so the first person on its list was elected to the seventh and last regional seat.

Scottish Labour Party	10
Scottish National Party	2
Scottish Socialist Party	2
Scottish Conservative and Unionist Party	1
Scottish Liberal Democrats	1
Scottish Green Party	1
Others:	0

Election Results 2003 for the Glasgow Region

Party	Constituency (FPTP)		Regional List		TOTAL		
	% of votes	% of seats	% of votes	% of seats	% of votes	No of seats	% of seats
Conservative	9	0	8	14	8	1	6
Labour	46	100	38	0	42	10	58
Lib Dems	9	0	7	14	8	1	6
SNP	19	0	18	29	18	2	12
SSP	15	0	15	29	14	2	12
BNP	0	0	1	0	1	0	0
Com PPDS	0	0	0	0	0	0	0
Pro Life	0	0	1	0	1	0	0
Green	0	0	7	14	4	1	6
SPA	0	0	0	0	0	0	0
SSCUP	0	0	2	0	1	0	0
Sc. Unionist	0	0	1	0	1	0	0
Soc.Lab.	0	0	2	0	1	0	0
UK Ind.P	0	0	0	0	0	0	0

All figures rounded to nearest whole per cent

4 HOW THE PARLIAMENT WORKS

INTRODUCTION

The supporters of the establishment of a Scottish Parliament frequently expressed the hope that such a body would be a new type of institution, with a new approach to the way that the business of government is carried on.[1] This chapter looks at the way in which that hope has been reflected in the reality of the arrangements made for the way the Parliament works. It considers in some detail the role of the Parliament's committees. It also looks at the opportunities that are available to MSPs to hold the Scottish Executive to account, and the way in which external individuals and organisations can influence the Parliament's work.

THE LEGISLATIVE FRAMEWORK

The Parliament is given a relatively free hand by the Scotland Act 1998 (SA 1998) in deciding how it should work. The Act does not set out detailed requirements for the Parliament's method of operation. It states that the proceedings of the Parliament will be regulated by standing orders.[2] Beyond that general requirement, there are only a small number of areas where the SA 1998 specifies what should be in the standing orders.

These statutory requirements contain important provisions about the passage of legislation, including procedures to ensure that the Parliament cannot make legislation on matters which are outside the powers given to it. These provisions are considered in the next chapter.

There are a number of other specific matters which the SA 1998 requires the Parliament to deal with in its standing orders, including rules to provide for the following[3]:

- the preservation of order in the Parliament's proceedings, including the prevention of criminal conduct or contempt of court during proceedings, and the prevention of the discussion of matters which are *sub judice*;
- the proceedings of the Parliament are to be held in public, except in certain specified circumstances;
- the Presiding Officer and his or her deputies are not all to come from the same political party;
- in the establishment of any committees and sub-committees, account must be taken of the balance of seats held by the different political parties in the Parliament.

---

[1] See, for example, Bernard Crick and David Millar *To Make the Parliament of Scotland a Model for Democracy* (1997).
[2] SA 1998, s 22.
[3] SA 1998, Sch 3.

The Standing Orders may also include rules allowing for the exclusion of MSPs from sittings of the Parliament and its committees and sub-committees, in certain circumstances.

It can be seen, therefore, that the SA 1998 lays down only broad guidelines for the operation of the Parliament, and in particular for how proposals for legislation should pass through the Parliament. The SA 1998 does not set out detailed guidelines for the way in which committees should operate, or for the number of stages that proposed legislation should pass through in Parliament.

STANDING ORDERS

Although the statutory requirements to be observed by the Parliament in deciding how it should function are relatively few, the Parliament operates within the framework of a comprehensive set of Standing Orders. In order that the Parliament would have Standing Orders in place when it commenced operation, its first Standing Orders were made by the Secretary of State for Scotland[4], using his powers to make transitional provisions for the Parliament. These transitional provisions were superseded in December 1999 when the Parliament adopted its own Standing Orders. The Parliament may, on a motion made by its Procedures Committee, amend its Standing Orders if an absolute majority of MSPs so decide[5] and the Parliament has subsequently made a number of quite substantial amendments to its original Standing Orders.

The Standing Orders are written in comparatively straightforward English and contain a glossary of terms, thus making them reasonably intelligible to members of the public. They cover such matters as meetings of the Parliament, elections to various posts within the Parliament and the Scottish Executive, the management of business, committees, the conduct of meetings, procedures for passing various types of Bills, subordinate legislation procedure, decisions and voting, statements and parliamentary questions, the laying and publication of documents, public access, petitions, the reporting of parliamentary proceedings, and miscellaneous matters.

The Standing Orders are modelled largely, although not completely, on the proposals made by the Consultative Steering Group on the Scottish Parliament (the 'CSG'). The CSG was set up by the UK Government early in 1998 to make proposals as to how the Parliament should carry out its business. It drew together representatives of all the major political parties along with other leading constitutional experts, and published its final report, 'Shaping Scotland's Parliament', in January 1999[6]. Its broad recommendations were endorsed by all the major political parties.

THE COMMITTEES OF THE PARLIAMENT

In most legislative assemblies, much of the detailed work is dealt with in committees rather than in a plenary session of all the body's members. The

---

[4] These can be found in the Schedule to the Scotland Act 1998 (Transitory and Transitional Provisions) (Standing Orders and Parliamentary Publications) Order 1999, SI 1999/1095.

[5] Rule 17.1 of the Standing Orders of the Scottish Parliament. (Subsequent references to Rules are references to the rules set out in these Standing Orders.)

[6] (1999) (referred to elsewhere in this book as the 'CSG Report').

arrangements for an assembly's committee structure are therefore a key aspect of its method of operation. This is particularly so in the case of the Scottish Parliament, where committees play a significant role in its activities. The CSG proposed a system of all-purpose 'subject' committees which combine the roles of both standing and select committees found at Westminster with broad remits which cover the consideration and scrutiny of both policy and proposals for legislation. The Parliament accepted this proposal. Standing Orders provide that the Parliament *may* establish such committees as it thinks fit, on a motion of the Parliamentary Bureau. Individual MSPs may also propose the establishment of subject committees. The CSG also recommended that certain 'mandatory' committees should be set up and, in the case of these, Standing Orders provide that the Parliament *must* establish them. In addition, whenever a Private Bill is introduced, the Parliament must establish a Private Bill Committee[7]. The Parliamentary Bureau proposes to the Parliament the establishment, membership, remit and duration of subject committees[8]. In practice, subject committees are normally established for the whole of the Parliament's four-year session.

Subject committees

Eight subject committees were initially established by the Parliament in 1999 and were given broad remits. The committees were as follows:

- Education, Culture and Sport
- Enterprise and Lifelong Learning
- Health and Community Care
- Justice and Home Affairs
- Local Government
- Rural Affairs (later renamed Rural Development)
- Social Inclusion, Housing and the Voluntary Sector (later renamed Social Justice)
- Transport and the Environment.

The workload of the Justice and Home Affairs Committee soon became so heavy that it was necessary to establish a second committee with an identical remit and the Committees are known as 'Justice 1' and 'Justice 2'.

After the elections in 2003, the subject committees (and their remits) were as follows:

- *Communities*: To consider and report on matters relating to anti-social behaviour, housing and area regeneration, poverty, voluntary sector issues, charity law and religious and faith organisations, and matters relating to the land use planning system and building standards, and such other matters as fall within the responsibility of the Minister for Communities.
- *Education and Young People*: To consider and report on matters relating to school and pre-school education and social work and such other

---

[7] Rule 9A.5.
[8] Rule 6.1.

matters relating to young people as fall within the responsibility of the
Minister for Education and Young People.

- *Enterprise and Culture* (including *Lifelong Learning, Tourism* and
  Sport): To consider and report on matters relating to the Scottish
  economy, business and industry, energy, training, further and higher
  education, lifelong learning and such other matters as fall within the
  responsibility of the Minister for Enterprise and Lifelong Learning; and
  matters relating to tourism, culture and sport and such other matters as
  fall within the responsibility of the Minister for Tourism, Culture and
  Sport.
- *Justice 1* and *Justice 2* share a common remit: To consider and report on
  matters relating to the administration of civil and criminal justice, the
  reform of the civil and criminal law and such other matters as fall within
  the responsibility of the Minister for Justice, and the functions of the
  Lord Advocate other than as head of the systems of criminal prosecution
  and investigations of deaths in Scotland.
- *Environment and Rural Development*: To consider and report on matters
  relating to rural development, environment and natural heritage, agriculture and fisheries and such other matters as fall within the responsibility of the Minister for Environment and Rural Development.
- *Health* (including *Community Care*): To consider and report on matters
  relating to health policy and the National Health Service in Scotland
  and such other matters as fall within the responsibility of the Minister
  for Health and Community Care.
- *Local Government and Transport*: To consider and report on matters
  relating to local government (including local government finance),
  cities and community planning and such other matters (excluding
  finance other than local government finance) which fall within the
  responsibility of the Minister for Finance and Public Services; and
  matters relating to transport which fall within the responsibility of the
  Minister for Transport.

Mandatory committees

Standing Orders prescribe the establishment and the remits of mandatory
committees[9]. They are:

- **Procedures Committee** which is to consider and report on the practice
  and procedures of the Parliament in relation to its business;
- **Standards Committee** which is to consider and report on the adoption,
  amendment and application of the code of conduct and on members'
  conduct in carrying out their Parliamentary duties. Where it considers it
  appropriate, the Standards Committee can recommend to the
  Parliament that a member's rights and privileges be withdrawn for a
  specified period[10];
- **Finance Committee** which is to consider and report on various aspects
  of public expenditure, any tax-varying resolution and on Budget Bills;

[9] Rule 6.1.5.
[10] Rule 6.5.2.

- **Audit Committee** which is to consider and report on financial control, accounting and auditing of public expenditure;
- **European and External Affairs Committee** which is to consider and report on proposals for and the implementation of EC legislation and on EC and EU issues generally;
- **Equal Opportunities Committee** which is to consider and report on matters relating to and the observance of equal opportunities within the Parliament;
- **Public Petitions Committee** which is to consider and report on whether a public petition is admissible and what action should be taken on petitions;
- **Subordinate Legislation Committee** which is to consider and report on matters relating to subordinate legislation and Scottish Statutory Instruments generally.

The Procedures, Standards and Finance Committees must be established within 21 sitting days of a general election and the other mandatory committees within 42 sitting days. Mandatory committees are established for the entire four-year session of the Parliament.

Most of the mandatory committees are concerned with organisational and procedural matters. It should be noted, however, that some of them, in particular the European and External Affairs Committee and Equal Opportunities Committee, have remits which in practice allow them also to deal with certain wider policy areas, similar to those which are dealt with by subject committees.

Ad hoc committees

The CSG also proposed that the Parliament should be able to set up ad hoc committees to allow consideration of issues on a broad basis, in order to deal with matters which cut across the conventional boundaries of government (for example, public health, social inclusion, and environmental sustainability). The Standing Orders do not make specific provision for such ad hoc committees, but they are sufficiently flexible to allow the establishment of such committees if the Parliament so wishes.

Remit of committees

A committee may consider any matter which is within its specific remit, or any other matter which is referred to it by the full Parliament or by any other committee. Where a matter is within its remit, or is otherwise referred to it, a committee can undertake a number of activities[11]. It can:

- consider the policy and administration of the Scottish Executive;
- consider any proposals for legislation, including both primary or secondary legislation, whether before the Scottish Parliament or the UK Parliament;
- consider any relevant EC legislation or international agreements or the like;

---

[11] See rule 6.2.

- consider whether there is a need for law reform in a particular area;
- initiate Bills for consideration by the Parliament;
- consider the financial proposals and financial administration of the Scottish Administration.

Composition of committees

Each committee has between 5 and 15 members. Members are appointed by the Parliament on a proposal from the Parliamentary Bureau[12]. Committees choose their own convener and deputy convener, but the Parliamentary Bureau recommends to the full Parliament the party from which they are to be appointed, and is required in so doing to have regard to the proportionate strength of the various parties in the Parliament. Committees normally meet in public unless the committee decides otherwise. When considering actual or potential proposals for legislation, a committee must meet in public unless it is taking evidence, when it can decide to meet in private. Committees can, with the approval of the Parliamentary Bureau and the full Parliament, establish their own sub-committees[13].

Ministers are not barred from becoming members of committees, but as matter of practice have not been appointed to either subject or mandatory committees. However, a Minister does have the right to participate (but not vote) in proceedings of a committee concerning proposals for legislation in the relevant subject area (as does the individual member concerned in the case of a Member's Bill), and in practice Ministers do, on occasion, attend relevant committees.

A committee may decide, with the approval of the Parliamentary Bureau and the Conveners' Group[14], to sit anywhere in Scotland, and a number of meetings have been held outside Edinburgh. However, the vast majority of committee meetings are held within the Parliament's own headquarters building in Edinburgh, notwithstanding the recommendation of the CSG that some committees should be permanently based outside Edinburgh 'to demonstrate that the Parliament is a Parliament for the whole of Scotland'.[15] Committees may appoint external advisers to assist them with their work[16], but the CSG recommendation that people who are not MSPs could be co-opted onto committees as non-voting members has not been incorporated into the Standing Orders. A committee may also appoint a 'reporter' to report to it on any matter within its remit[17]. This allows the Scottish Parliament to make use of the *rapporteur* system extensively used in the European Parliament and elsewhere, where such a person draws up a draft report for a committee. It was envisaged by the CSG that a *rapporteur* would act as a focal point for interest groups and individuals wishing to make representations to a committee. Parliamentary committees have begun to make use of the power to appoint a reporter, although, as yet, such an appointment does not seem to have acquired the influence which can be wielded by a *rapporteur* in the European system.

---

[12] Rule 6.3.1.
[13] See Chapter 12 of the Rules for the detailed provisions for Committee Procedures.
[14] For the conveners' group see below.
[15] Rule 12.3.2; CSG Information Paper CSG (98)(92).
[16] Rule 12.7. A number of committees have made use of the power to appoint advisers.
[17] Rule 12.6.

Committee substitutes

Any political party which has five or more members of the Parliament may nominate a member of the party to be a substitute for the members of the party on a particular committee[18]. The committee substitutes act in the place of any member of the same party who is unable to act because of illness, family circumstances, adverse weather conditions, a requirement to attend to other business in the Parliament or urgent constituency business. Committee substitutes are appointed for the duration of the relevant committee unless the membership of their political party group subsequently falls below five.

Conveners' group

A Conveners' Group[19] has been set up which is not technically a committee. It consists of the Presiding Officer and the conveners of the subject and the mandatory committees. Its functions include making recommendations as to the operation of the committees and to approve (along with the Parliamentary Bureau) the location of committee meetings and travel outside the UK of committee members in connection with their committees' remits.

The committees have been described as 'the Parliament's powerhouse'[20]. Their workload has turned out to be much heavier than was originally envisaged. They play a very active role in the Parliament's business, gathering information, scrutinising the policy of departments, holding inquiries and scrutinising primary and secondary legislative proposals. They can also initiate Bills[21]. Committees can and have made important changes to Bills as they progress through the various stages towards the statute book[22] and have shown considerable independence from the Executive. Committee members develop expertise in the policy areas within their committee's remit and in general act in a less adversarial way than they do at meetings of the full Parliament.

Cross-party groups

Cross-party groups are groups which consist of MSPs from each of the main political parties represented in the Parliament. They provide an opportunity for MSPs and members of the public and outside organisations to meet and discuss a shared interest in a particular subject or cause and around fifty of them were formed during the life of the first Parliament. Examples of cross-party groups which have been established are the Animal Welfare Group, the Chronic Pain Group, the Palestine Group, and the Group on Refugees and Asylum Seekers. As these groups may be able to gain some influence within the Parliament, it was considered imperative that rules of good practice should be set down for their

---

[18] Rule 6.3A.

[19] Rule 6A.1.

[20] Barry Winetrobe *Realising the Vision: a Parliament with a Purpose* (The Constitution Unit, October 2001).

[21] For Committee Bills see ch 5.

[22] Committees made significant changes to the Public Appointments and Public Bodies etc (Scotland) Act 2003.

operation. Each group must apply to the Standards Committee for recognition and only groups approved by that Committee are entitled to call themselves Cross-Party groups of the Scottish Parliament and to have access to Parliamentary facilities. Section 8 of the code of conduct sets out the framework of rules for their operation.

THE PARLIAMENTARY BUREAU

A particularly important role in the management of the Parliament's business is played by its Parliamentary Bureau. The Bureau operates under special rules set out in the Standing Orders and, although clearly a committee of the Parliament, it is governed by different rules from those which apply to other committees.[23] The Bureau is comprised of the Presiding Officer, and one representative of each party with five or more MSPs (nominated by the Parliamentary leader of that party). In addition, members of parties with fewer than five MSPs, or independents, can combine together to form a group of five or more members for the purpose of appointing a representative to the Bureau. Members of the Bureau vote on a 'weighted basis', where they wield one vote for each MSP their party has in the full Parliament.

The main functions of the Parliamentary Bureau are to:

- recommend to the Parliament its business programme;
- recommend the establishment, remit, membership, and duration of any committee or sub-committee of the Parliament;
- decide any issue as to whether a matter comes within the responsibility of a particular committee, and to decide which committee should be the 'lead committee' where an issue falls within the responsibility of more than one committee.

The Presiding Officer chairs meetings of the Bureau, but has no vote, unless there is a tie, when he or she can use a casting vote. A deputy Presiding Officer chairs the meeting in the absence of the Presiding Officer. Meetings of the Bureau are held in private, although it can if it wishes invite other MSPs to participate in a meeting, on a non-voting basis.

HOLDING THE EXECUTIVE TO ACCOUNT

As well as making laws, most parliamentary assemblies have the important role of monitoring how governments implement the law once made, and how they carry out their functions in general. As with many other activities, the SA 1998 places no statutory requirements on the Parliament as to how it should go about the task of holding the executive arm of government to account. However, reflecting a widely held view that effective scrutiny of the Scottish Executive should be incorporated into the practice of the Parliament, the CSG made detailed proposals on how such accountability could be put into effect[24]. The Standing Orders eventually adopted by the Parliament are broadly based upon the CSG proposals,

---

[23] See Rules, Ch 5.
[24] CSG Report, 3.4.

although they are not quite as comprehensive as envisaged by the CSG. The following opportunities to ensure such accountability are available to the Parliament:

- MSPs may submit questions for either an oral or a written answer by a member of the Scottish Executive[25]. Questions for oral answer are submitted in writing in advance but supplementary questions of which no notice has been given are permitted. Question Time lasts for up to 40 minutes each week (normally on Thursdays) and First Minister's Question Time lasts for up to 20 minutes immediately following Question Time.
- The First Minister may, if he or she so wishes, make a statement to the Parliament outlining the proposed policy objectives and the legislative programme of the Scottish Executive for the Parliamentary year ahead, and if such a statement is made it will be debated by the Parliament[26]. This provision is optional, however, rather than mandatory, as the CSG seemed to suggest should be the case. (Neither was the CSG recommendation that after each election the Parliament should debate the four-year legislative programme of the newly formed Scottish Executive incorporated into the Standing Orders, although such a debate was held after the Labour–Liberal Democrat coalition was formed in 1999 and again in 2003.)
- Debates on general policy issues can be held from time to time, and a specified number of days are reserved for debates initiated by committees and opposition parties.
- At the end of each meeting of the Parliament there is a period of up to 45 minutes for individual MSPs' business[27].
- A motion of no confidence in either the entire Scottish Executive or an individual Minister can be tabled by any MSP, and if it is supported by at least 25 members, it must be debated[28]. (It would appear, however, that as the SA 1998 provides for only the resignation of the Scottish Executive *en bloc* following a no confidence vote, only a vote of no confidence in the entire Executive would be binding. A vote of no confidence in an individual Minister would seem to be advisory only (although no doubt such a vote would be most telling.)
- A Minister can participate in the work of a committee when it is considering that Minister's legislative proposals and such participation gives the committee members a further opportunity to scrutinise the activity of the Scottish Executive.

THE PRESIDING OFFICER

It will be seen from other sections of this book that the Parliament's Presiding Officer plays an important part in its activities. Under the statutory provisions of

---

[25] See Ch 13 of the Rules on Statements and Parliamentary Questions.
[26] Rule 5.7.
[27] Rule 5.6.
[28] See r 8.12 and the SA 1998, ss 45, 47, 48 and 49.

the SA 1998, he or she has a very important part to play in the procedure whereby proposed legislation passes through the Parliament[29]. The Standing Orders give further important responsibilities to the Presiding Officer[30]. These include the duty to:

- preside over plenary meetings of the Parliament;
- convene and chair the Parliamentary Bureau;
- interpret and apply the Standing Orders;
- represent the Parliament in discussions and exchanges with any parliamentary, governmental, administrative or other body, whether within or outwith the UK.

The SA 1998 provides that the Parliament must elect a Presiding Officer and two deputies, who should not all represent the same party. In the first parliament, the Presiding Officer was David Steel who had been elected as a Liberal Democrat; in the second Parliament, elected in 2003, the Presiding Officer is George Reid, elected as an SNP member. The Deputy Presiding Officers elected in 2003 were from the Labour and the Conservative groups. Once elected to the office, the Presiding Officer and his deputies[31] are expected to put aside party politics and act impartially on behalf of all the members of the Parliament. The Standing Orders further provide that the Presiding Officer and the deputy Presiding Officers have casting votes in the event of a tie in a plenary meeting of the Parliament (except where there is a tie in a vote for First Minister, Presiding Officer and deputies, and members of the Parliamentary corporation), or in a meeting of the Parliamentary Bureau. The Presiding Officer does not otherwise have a vote[32], but the deputies have normal voting rights except when actually presiding over Parliamentary business. To be appointed, each of the Presiding Officer and deputies must obtain an absolute majority of those MSPs actually voting in that election[33], but, once appointed, can be removed only by an absolute majority of all MSPs[34]. The Presiding Officer has a basic salary of £37,056, plus the MSP's allowance of £49,315, while the Deputy Presiding Officers have a basic salary of £23,210, plus the MSP's allowance.[35]

The Standing Orders specifically require the Presiding Officer and deputies when exercising their functions to 'act impartially, taking account of the interests of all members equally'[36]. Nevertheless, the functions of the posts have the potential, particularly in the case of the Presiding Officer, to give their holders considerable influence over the business of the Parliament. The degree to which that proves to be the case no doubt depends on the personality of the person elected to the post, and the political balance between the parties represented in the Parliament. Since the electoral system makes it unlikely that there will ever be one party holding a clear majority of seats in the Parliament and that, accordingly,

---

[29] See ch 5.

[30] See Ch 3 of the Rules for the detailed provisions applicable to the Presiding Officer and deputy Presiding Officers.

[31] When elected the Presiding Officer puts aside all political affiliation, the deputy officers do so only when called on to preside.

[32] Rule 11.5.5.

[33] See r 11.9.10.

[34] Rule 3.5.

[35] 2003 figures.

[36] Rule 3.1.3.

there will be a greater role for inter-party bargaining, there is a reasonable possibility that the office of Presiding Officer is one which will have, on a continuing basis, a public profile, and perhaps also degree of political influence, greater than its Westminster counterpart.

SCOTTISH PARLIAMENTARY CORPORATE BODY (SPCB)

A brief mention should be made of the Scottish Parliamentary Corporate Body, which is established by the SA 1998[37]. The principal function of this body, described in the Parliament's Standing Orders as the 'Parliamentary Corporation', is to provide the Parliament with the property, staff and services it requires. This includes the staff who service committees, parliamentary researchers and librarians, and other ancillary staff. It makes decisions on a wide range of issues concerning the running of the Parliament, including the financing of the Parliament and the allocation of the budget, accommodation, the use and security of parliamentary facilities, and the building of the new permanent Parliament at Holyrood. The SPCB is also responsible for the preparation of the Parliament's Official Report and its Journal (see below). It also arranges for the broadcasting of the Parliament's proceedings, subject to a code of conduct set down by the full Parliament[38]. The establishment of the SPCB ensures that these services are provided independently of the Scottish Executive. The members of the SPCB, who direct its operation (subject to the Parliament's rights to give directions to it) are the Presiding Officer and four other MSPs. It was not envisaged by the CSG that these members would be appointed on a political basis but the Standing Orders say nothing on this point, and in fact the four main parties in the Parliament agreed amongst themselves that they would each appoint one member of the SPCB when the first appointments to the body were made.

Any legal proceedings by or against the Parliament, its Presiding Officer or deputies, or any of its staff, are carried out by or against the SPCB on their behalf[39]. The SPCB is treated as a Crown body for the purposes of a number of important statutes, and given the privileges of such a body[40].

PUBLIC ACCOUNTABILITY, OPENNESS AND ACCESSIBILITY

Investigating complaints

As outlined above, the key principles adopted by the CSG include an emphasis on the Parliament being open and accountable to the wider Scottish public. The only provision of the SA 1998 giving any rights to the public over the system of government in Scotland is that requiring the Parliament to set up a system to investigate complaints made by members of the public to MSPs alleging mal-administration by members of the Scottish Executive or any other member of the Scottish Administration (or any one acting on their behalf, including of course civil servants)[41]. That provision is modelled on the existing UK Parliamentary

---

[37] SA 1998, s 21.
[38] See rr 16.2–16.4.
[39] SA 1998, s 40.
[40] Scottish Parliamentary Corporate Body (Crown Status) Order 1999, SI 1999/677.
[41] SA 1998, s 91.

Ombudsman system, and the obligation to set up such a system is restricted to complaints of the kind which that UK official is required to investigate (in essence, complaints of maladministration by government departments, but excluding a number of matters such as the investigation of crime and commercial transactions)[42].

However, the SA 1998 allows the Parliament, if it wishes, to set up a wider investigatory system, including amongst others: the investigation of any action taken by or on behalf of the Scottish Parliamentary Corporate Body, any action taken by or on behalf of any Scottish public authority with mixed functions or no reserved functions, and any action concerning Scotland, and not relating to reserved matters, which is taken by or on behalf of a cross-border public authority[43]. It appears to be open to the Parliament to decide whether or not complaints made under any such wider investigatory system would have to be made through MSPs, in contrast with the 'Ombudsman' system which the Parliament has a legal duty to establish.

Initial arrangements for an Ombudsman for the Scottish Parliament were put in place by the Secretary of State for Scotland under his powers to make transitional arrangements under the SA 1998[44]. These set up the office of Scottish Parliamentary Commissioner for Administration, with powers and procedures modelled very much on the existing counterpart at UK Parliamentary level. The Ombudsman appointed under these arrangements was the person who was the UK Parliamentary Commissioner for Administration at the time.

The transitional arrangements continued until 2002 when the Parliament passed the Scottish Public Services Ombudsman Act. This Act went much further than the establishment of a Scottish Parliamentary Ombudsman, and created a 'one-stop shop' for the investigation of complaints against much of the devolved public sector in Scotland, by combining the offices of the Scottish Parliamentary Commissioner for Administration, the Health Service Ombudsman for Scotland, the Local Government Ombudsman for Scotland and the Housing Association Ombudsman for Scotland and certain other complaints mechanisms.

Although the SA 1998 envisaged that all complaints of maladministration at Scottish Executive level would be channelled through an MSP (the MSP filter), the Scottish Public Services Act 2002 does not contain such a restriction and complaints can be submitted directly by members of the public.

The Public Services Ombudsman and three deputies took up office in the autumn of 2002[45].

Public petitions

Meaningful participation by the people of Scotland in the work of the Scottish Parliament was seen by the Scottish Constitutional Convention and the CSG as a key element of the operation of the Parliament. Both bodies recommended that the Standing Orders should enable members of the public to petition the Parliament. The Public Petitions Committee is one of the mandatory committees

---

[42] See Parliamentary Commissioner Act 1967, Sch 3.
[43] SA 1998, s 91(3).
[44] Scotland Act 1998 (Transitory and Transitional Provisions) (Complaints of Maladministration) Order 1999, SI 1999/1351.
[45] For more on the Scottish Public Services Ombudsman see: www.scottishombudsman.org.uk.

which the Parliament is required to establish under its Standing Orders[46]. Standing Orders also set out the procedures for bringing a petition to the attention of the Parliament[47]. A petition may be presented by an individual, a body corporate or an unincorporated association of persons, either through an MSP or directly to the Parliament. Petitions should contain the name and address of the petitioner and those of anyone supporting the petition. There is, however, no requirement that a certain minimum number of signatures be obtained in support of the petition (as is the norm in many assemblies elsewhere in Europe[48]). Originally Standing Orders required the petition to be in English, but that is now no longer the case. The petition may be lodged in writing with the Clerk of the Parliament or sent to the Clerk by email. There is also a facility for the electronic submission of petitions via an interactive form on the Parliament's website[49]. The Clerk then sends it as soon as possible to the Public Petitions Committee.

After arranging for the petition to be translated into English, if necessary, if the Committee decides that the Scottish Parliament has the power to deal with the matter raised by the petition, it can deal with it in a number of ways. It can: refer the petition to the Scottish Ministers or any other appropriate body or person for information or consideration; refer it to the relevant subject committee; prepare a report for consideration by the Parliamentary Bureau or by the Parliament itself; or take any other action which the Committee considers to be appropriate. The Committee may also meet outside Edinburgh to hear presentations of petitions. The petitioner must be notified, if necessary in a language other than English, of the action taken by the Committee[50].

In the first four-year session of the Parliament, the Public Petitions Committee considered 615 petitions, covering a wide range of subjects including housing, transport, the protection of heritage sites, genetically modified crops and many others. The Committee hears presentations on a large number of the petitions (including one which involved a video-link to the Shetland Isles) and is clearly fulfilling its role as a gateway for public involvement in the parliamentary process[51].

Consultation

The CSG also emphasised that prior to legislation being submitted to the Parliament, there should be extensive consultation with organisations and individuals outside the Parliament. To achieve this, as described below[52], it recommended that legislative proposals from the Scottish Executive should be accompanied by a memorandum showing what public consultation has been undertaken, and the Standing Orders provide that such details must be included in a 'Policy Memorandum'[53].

---

[46] Rule 6.1.

[47] Rule 15.4.

[48] Eg Germany and Italy. See ch 4 of the report 'Parliamentary Practices in Devolved Parliaments' (Centre for Scottish Public Policy for the Scottish Office, 1998).

[49] www.scottish.parliament.uk/e-petitions/index.htm.

[50] Rule 15.6.

[51] In the first eight months of its operation, the Parliament considered more than 90 petitions, some emanating from particularly active petitioners who lodged petitions on various different issues (in the case of at least one petitioner, causing the Public Petitions Committee some concern as to how it could deal with the volume of his petitions!).

[52] See ch 5.

[53] Rule 9.3.3(c)(ii).

The CSG also suggested that there might be a role for forums bringing together particular interest groups, eg a Civic Forum, a Business Forum, and a Youth Forum[54]. Proposals to establish the Civic Forum were announced by the Scottish Executive towards the end of 1999. The Civic Forum is made up of a diverse range of organisation in Scottish life – trade unions, churches, non-governmental organisations, national and local charities, business and professional organisations. The aim of the Forum is to build a new culture of active citizenship in which the people of Scotland have an opportunity to be involved in influencing government policies. It is mainly funded by the Scottish Executive, from which it received £200,000 in 2003.

A Scottish Youth Parliament was launched in 1999 and has a membership of around 200 elected young people aged between 14 and 25. The Youth Parliament meets three times a year, discusses issues which affect young people across Scotland and tries to propose solutions to these issues. It too is supported financially by the Scottish Executive.

The Scottish Parliament Business Exchange was set up in November 2001 with the aim of bringing the Parliament and the business community closer together in a non-partisan and non-lobbying way. It has been registered as an educational charity and has a board which consists of parliamentarians, people with business and related interests and a representative of the Scottish Trades Union Congress. The main funding for this organisation comes from membership subscriptions

Public access

The meetings of the Parliament and its committees and sub-committees are held in public, with very few exceptions. Members of the public are admitted to the large public gallery during any meeting of the Parliament and visits by students and school parties are catered for. Access to the chamber itself is limited to MSPs, the Lord Advocate and Solicitor General for Scotland, to persons authorised by the Presiding Officer or Clerk and to persons invited by the Parliament to attend or to address the Parliament[55]. The Parliament has been addressed by, among others, the Queen, the Prime Minister and the President of the European Parliament.

Use of language

The wish to ensure that the Parliament is seen to represent the whole of Scotland is seen in the provision made in Standing Orders that, although the Parliament should normally conduct its business in English, members may also speak in Scots Gaelic or any other language with the agreement of the Presiding Officer as may persons addressing the Parliament on the invitation of the Parliament[56].

However, although interpretation facilities are provided within the building, the Parliament does not have its own interpreters available on a permanent basis, and those wishing to speak in a language other than English are required to give 24 hours' notice in order to ensure that interpreters can be provided. Moreover, there is no automatic provision for MSPs' speeches to be interpreted into English from

[54] CSG Report, 2.38.
[55] Rules 15.1–15.3.
[56] Rule 7.1.

Gaelic or any other language. Accordingly, it is not possible for languages other than English to be used on a day-to-day basis, and it may be thought that the provision to allow the use of Gaelic is more of symbolic significance rather than practical utility for the normal business of the Parliament. However, a number of documents published by the Scottish Parliament are made available in Gaelic, including the Parliament's Annual Report; and both Gaelic and English are used in the Parliament's website.

'Family-friendly' hours of business

The Parliament also adopted the suggestion of the CSG that it should avoid the long-standing Westminster practice of starting parliamentary sittings in the afternoons and continuing them until late at night. Instead the Scottish Parliament has what are described as 'family-friendly' hours of business. The Standing Orders lay down that the Parliament will normally sit on Monday afternoons (to enable MSPs to travel from their constituencies on Monday morning), from Tuesday to Thursday from 9.30 am to 5.30 pm and on Friday mornings (to enable MSPs to travel back in the afternoon)[57]. It was hoped that these hours would encourage people with family responsibilities to consider standing for election. In addition, when considering what weeks the Parliament should be in recess, the Parliament Bureau is obliged to take account of the dates when schools in any part of Scotland are to be on holiday. This is in stark contrast to Westminster which continues in session well into July despite the fact that Scottish school summer holidays start at the end of June.

Reporting of proceedings and other publications

The standing orders also deal with the reporting of the proceedings of the Parliament and its committees[58]. The clerks draw up minutes of each meeting of the Parliament and its committees, recording all the items of business taken at any meeting, the results of any decisions taken and of any divisions or elections which took place. The minutes are printed and published as soon as possible. In addition, a substantially verbatim report of proceedings is made which contains all the contributions made in the Parliament and in committees both by MSPs and by any other speakers such as expert witnesses. It also contains all written questions together with the answers. This report is known as the Scottish Parliament Official Report and is the equivalent of Hansard in the Westminster Parliament. There are also arrangements for the broadcasting of the proceedings of the Parliament and its committees.

Standing Orders also provide for a Journal of the Scottish Parliament to be printed and published at intervals, containing minutes, notice of Bills and Scottish Statutory Instruments and notice of reports by committees to the Parliament. However, at the time of writing, no edition of the Journal had been produced.

In addition to the publications of proceedings covered by the Standing Orders, the Parliament produces a large number of other documents which are available to the public. These include the daily Business Bulletin which details the business of

---

[57] Rule 2.2.
[58] Rules 16.1–16.5.

the day, committee agendas, questions, motions and amendments and petitions lodged. There is also a weekly publication called WHISP (What's Happening in the Scottish Parliament) which provides more general information on the work of the Parliament. From time to time briefing papers are published by SPICe (the Scottish Parliament Information Centre) covering topics such as the Holyrood building project, the Legal Basis of Scottish Banknotes and Gender in the Scottish Parliament.

An Annual Report of the Scottish Parliament is published (in English and Gaelic) as well as an annual Statistical Report.

Both the Scottish Executive and the Scottish Parliament have websites[59].

---

[59] The addresses are www.scotland.gov.uk and www.scottish.parliament.uk respectively.

5 MAKING LAWS

INTRODUCTION

The Scottish Parliament has the power to make laws. As we have seen in chapter 2, the areas in which it is able to exercise that law-making power are wide. This chapter looks at the way in which proposals for legislation proceed through the Parliament, taking into account the mechanisms put in place both by the Scotland Act 1998 (SA 1998) and by the Parliament's Standing Orders to ensure that the Parliament does not make legislation in areas outside its field of responsibility.

The way in which the Parliament deals with legislation is similar in many respects to the way in which legislation is dealt with by the Westminster Parliament at present. In the Scottish Parliament, just as at Westminster, a proposal for legislation – a 'Bill' – is normally considered both by a committee and the full Parliament. At the end of the process, a Bill must receive Royal Assent before it can become law. When it has done so, it becomes an 'Act of the Scottish Parliament' or 'asp'[1]. In addition to Acts which are made by the Parliament in that way, a great deal of subordinate legislation is made by Scottish Ministers[2].

However, there are also important differences between the Scottish and the UK systems. First of all, there is no second chamber in the Scottish Parliament, unlike at Westminster where Bills have to pass through the House of Lords as well as the House of Commons. Second, the Scottish Parliament and the Scottish Executive have some limited power to take part in the law-making procedure in areas which do not otherwise fall within the Parliament's remit. And, perhaps most significantly, as the Parliament is restricted in its powers to make laws, the process whereby laws are made by it includes a number of features designed to ensure that the Parliament does not make laws in areas where it is not permitted to do so.

In this field, as in many others, the statutory requirements laid down in the SA 1998 were fleshed out in some detail by the CSG in its report, *Shaping Scotland's Parliament*, and subsequently embodied in the Parliament's Standing Orders[3]. In this chapter, the statutory provisions for Bills to pass through the Parliament are examined, and the procedures set out in Standing Orders are then looked at in some detail. Thereafter, the procedures for subordinate legislation are examined.

SCRUTINY OF BILLS TO ENSURE LEGISLATIVE COMPETENCE

Detailed provisions are built into the SA 1998 to ensure that each Bill is subjected to scrutiny to prevent the creeping in of any provision which is outside the powers

---

[1] SPA 1998, s 28.

[2] See pp 81–82.

[3] The first Standing Orders for the Scottish Parliament were made by a statutory instrument of the UK Parliament (SI 1999/1095). In December 1999, the Parliament resolved to adopt its own Standing Orders. These are largely based on the Standing Orders made by SI 1999/1095. The rules relating to the procedures for Bills are set out in Ch 9 of the Standing Orders. (Subsequent references to Rules are references to the rules set out in the Standing Orders.)

of the Scottish Parliament. This process of scrutiny begins even before a Bill is considered by the Parliament. On the introduction of a Bill into the Parliament, the Presiding Officer must provide a written statement which indicates whether or not, in his view, the provisions of the Bill are within the legislative competence of the Parliament. If he thinks that any of the provisions are not within the competence of the Parliament, he must indicate what those provisions are and the reasons for his view. However, the fact that the Presiding Officer takes the view that provisions of a Bill are outwith legislative competence does not prevent the Bill being introduced. If the Bill is an Executive Bill, the member of the Scottish Executive in charge of it should also consider the matter and make a written statement to the Parliament that the Bill is within that legislative competence[4]. Both take legal advice before making such a statement.

After a Bill has been passed by the Parliament, certain Law Officers – the Advocate General for Scotland, the Lord Advocate[5] and the Attorney-General – also have a role in the scrutiny of Bills. If one of them has doubts as to whether any provision is within the legislative competence of the Parliament, he or she can refer the matter to the Judicial Committee of the Privy Council[6] for a decision.[7] By contrast with the statement required before or at the time of the introduction of a Bill, this power to make a reference can only be exercised *after* a Bill has been passed by the Parliament. Such a reference has to be made within four weeks of the Bill being passed by the Parliament and during that period the Presiding Officer must not submit the Bill for Royal Assent unless the Law Officers have waived their rights to make a reference. If the Judicial Committee decides that any provision of the Bill is not within the legislative competence of the Parliament, the Presiding Officer is not permitted to submit it in its unamended form for Royal Assent. Instead, the Bill returns to the Parliament which may reconsider the Bill and amend it so as to resolve the problem[8]. If the Law Officers waive their rights to challenge the Bill, the Presiding Officer can submit the Bill for Royal Assent before four weeks have elapsed. Since the UK joined the European Community, it has been possible for UK courts to refer certain questions relating to the interpretation of EC law to the European Court of Justice (ECJ) for a preliminary ruling. If a matter has been referred to the Judicial Committee of the Privy Council by one of the Law Officers, the Judicial Committee may make a further reference to the ECJ. Section 34 allows for the withdrawal of the reference if the Parliament decides that it wishes to reconsider the Bill.

Secretaries of State in the UK Government also have the power to intervene[9]. Any one of them may make an order prohibiting the Presiding Officer from submitting a Bill for Royal Assent in two sets of circumstances: first, where a Secretary of State believes that any provision would be incompatible with any international obligations (other than obligations under EC treaties, or arising from the European Convention on Human Rights), or the interests of defence or national security; and, second, where a Secretary of State believes that the Bill contains provisions which will modify the law as it relates to reserved matters *and* there are reasonable grounds to believe that the modification will have an adverse

---

[4] SA 1998, s 31.
[5] See pp 78–79.
[6] See ch 7.
[7] SA 1998, s 33.
[8] SA 1998, s 36.
[9] SA 1998, s 35.

effect on the operation of the law as it applies to reserved matters. As mentioned[10], the Parliament does have a limited power to pass laws which affect matters reserved to the Westminster Parliament. The power given to a Secretary of State to prohibit legislation being submitted for Royal Assent allows the UK Government to prevent such legislation reaching the statute book. Like the Law Officers, a Secretary of State has only four weeks after the passing of a Bill in which to decide whether to intervene and prohibit it from becoming law and similarly may waive that right. Again, where such an order is made by a Secretary of State, the Parliament can reconsider the Bill and amend it to remove the offending provisions

It should be noted that the power to make an order can be exercised by *any* UK Secretary of State. It can be envisaged that it might be the Secretary of State with the relevant departmental interest who actually exercises the power (for example, in the first case, the Foreign Secretary); but no doubt political factors will also have a part to play in the decision as to which Secretary of State exercises the power. For example, the UK Government might consider it politically preferable for this supervisory power over the Scottish Parliament to be exercised by the Secretary of State for Scotland or any successor office. In practice it is the Secretary of State for Scotland who is informed on each occasion the Parliament passes a Bill.

As has been mentioned above, the Law Officers and Secretaries of State can inform the Presiding Officer, at any time, that they do not intend to intervene to prevent a Bill becoming law. If they do so, they cannot then change their minds and intervene later to prevent the Bill receiving the Royal Assent but if a Bill is approved by the Parliament after reconsideration, the Law Officers and Secretaries of State have a further four-week opportunity to intervene again

THE STAGES OF BILLS

In the UK Parliament, a Bill has to go through a cumbersome process in both the House of Commons and the House of Lords before it can receive Royal Assent and become an Act of Parliament. The stages in each House are:

- first reading
- second reading
- committee stage
- report stage
- third reading.

The pressures of time in the House of Commons are enormous. It is quite common for important clauses in Bills (including the Scotland Bill) to receive little or no scrutiny by MPs. The pace of business in the House of Lords is much more leisurely and one of their roles in the legislative process is that of scrutiny and amendment so that any ambiguities and anomalies in a Bill may be removed.

The arrangements made for the scrutiny of Bills in the Scottish Parliament are designed to simplify the process considerably compared with Westminster. The arrangements in the Scottish Parliament also give the Parliament's committees a more prominent role and increase the opportunities for participation by the public.

---

[10] See ch 2.

The SA 1998 lays down that a Bill should normally pass through the following stages in the Parliament[11]:

- a general debate on a Bill with an opportunity for MSPs to vote on its general principles;
- consideration by MSPs of the details of the Bill (including an opportunity to vote on those details);
- a final stage at which a Bill can be passed or rejected.

The Parliament's Standing Orders give effect to these requirements by specifying three stages for all Public Bills, namely Stage 1, Stage 2 and Stage 3. The Standing Orders also set out the minimum period of time which should elapse between Stages 1 and 2 and between Stages 2 and 3.

However, Standing Orders also allow for an emergency measure to pass through all the stages in the Parliament more quickly (although it is still subject to the scrutiny procedures described above)[12]. In addition, in the case of Private Bills (see below) and certain Bills of primarily a formal nature, the Parliament may use a different procedure from that set out above[13].

The Parliament's Standing Orders are also required by the SA 1998 to cater for the situation that would arise if the Judicial Committee has decided that a provision in a Bill goes beyond the legislative competence of the Parliament, or a Secretary of State has intervened to prevent the Bill being submitted for Royal Assent, as described above[14]. In either set of circumstances, the Parliament is required to reconsider the Bill in question. This reconsideration stage enables the MSPs to remove the offending provisions and bring the Bill within the legislative competence of the Parliament, or, as appropriate, deal with the concerns relating to international obligations or defence and national security. At the end of this stage, the Bill can again be approved or rejected.

The SA 1998, therefore, only lays down the basic framework for the passage of Bills through the Parliament. The Parliament is given a great deal of freedom to regulate its own procedure in this respect, but here, as in other areas, the CSG proposals offered a model on which the Parliament's Standing Orders were based.

CONSULTATION

As the Parliament has no second House to act as a revising chamber, care has to be taken before a Bill starts on its progress to ensure that ambiguities and anomalies are removed as far as possible. The CSG recognised this difficulty, and in its report it recommended that legislative proposals go through an extensive consultation procedure both before their introduction into the Parliament and as they go through the legislative process. Such consultation serves to provide an opportunity for such ambiguities and anomalies to be identified, and also to meet the political objectives of ensuring maximum public involvement in the Parliament's work, of securing agreement (so far as is possible) on policy and of airing substantive issues and objections.

---

[11] SA 1998, s 36.
[12] Rule 9.21.
[13] Rules 9.17–9.20.
[14] Rule 9.9.

The CSG emphasised that the consultation process should consist of more than an invitation to submit comments on specific legislative proposals. Accordingly, it recommended that legislative proposals from the Scottish Executive should have completed a consultative process before they are presented to the Parliament. It suggested that the Scottish Minister responsible for an area of policy should inform the relevant Committee of the Executive's intentions in its area of interest, and should discuss with it the relevant bodies to be involved in the consultation process. In order to ensure that the consultative procedure had been carried out, it recommended that the Parliament's Standing Orders should require a Bill when introduced to the Parliament by the Executive to be accompanied by a memorandum giving details of the consultative process undertaken in that case. That would allow the committee concerned to arrange for further consultation if it felt that the Executive's consultation had been insufficient. In practice, however, quite a few Bills have been introduced by the Scottish Executive with virtually no prior consultation.

THE PASSAGE OF BILLS THROUGH THE PARLIAMENT

There are three main types of Public Bills, namely Executive Bills, Committee Bills and Members' Bills. The Scottish Parliament may also pass Private Bills, but these are relatively uncommon.

As described above, the SA 1998 requires Bills normally to go through three stages. If a Bill is rejected at Stage 1 or Stage 3 (it cannot be rejected at Stage 2), no further proceedings are to be taken on the Bill and a Bill in the same or similar terms may not be introduced within six months of the date on which it was rejected. A Bill falls if it has not been passed by the end of the session in which it was introduced, but a Bill in the same or similar terms may be introduced in the following session. A session of the Scottish Parliament is the four-year period from one general election to the next.

Executive Bills

A Bill is introduced by being lodged with the clerks by the member in charge of the Bill. It must be in the proper form, be signed by the member introducing it and it may also be signed by other MSPs who support it[15]. On introduction, a Bill must be accompanied by a written statement by the Presiding Officer which indicates whether or not in his view the provisions of the Bill are within the legislative competence of the Parliament. If there are provisions which would be outwith the Parliament's legislative competence, he must indicate what these provisions are and give reasons for his view[16]. The Bill must also be accompanied by a Financial Memorandum which sets out the best estimates of costs to which the provisions of the Bill would give rise and the best estimates of the timescales over which these costs could be expected to arise. The Financial Memorandum must distinguish separately costs which could fall on the Scottish Administration, Scottish local authorities and other bodies, individuals and businesses[17].

An Executive Bill, which is a Bill introduced by a member of the Scottish Executive, must also have several other accompanying documents. These are:

---

[15] Rule 9.2.
[16] Rule 9.3.1. This is part of the pre-legislative scrutiny of a Bill. See pp 54–56.
[17] Rule 9.3.2.

- a statement signed by the member of the Scottish Executive in charge of the Bill which states that in his or her view the provisions of the Bill would be within the legislative competence of the Parliament[18];
- explanatory notes which summarise objectively what each of the provisions of the Bill does and any other information necessary to explain the effect of the Bill;
- a policy memorandum which sets out –
  - the policy objectives of the Bill;
  - whether alternative ways of meeting those objectives were considered and, if so, why the approach in the Bill was adopted;
  - the consultation, if any, which was undertaken on the Bill's objectives and the ways of meeting them and a summary of the outcome of the consultation;
  - an assessment of the effects, if any, of the Bill on equal opportunities, human rights, island communities, local government, sustainable development and any other matter which the Scottish Ministers consider relevant[19].

If the Bill contains any provision which charges expenditure on the Scottish Consolidated Fund there must also be an accompanying report signed by the Auditor General stating whether, in his view, the charge is appropriate[20]. So far, no such statement has been required.

Once a Bill has been introduced and printed, it is referred by the Parliamentary Bureau[21] to the committee of the Parliament within whose remit the subject matter of the Bill falls. This committee is known as 'the lead committee' and it is the task of the lead committee to consider and report on the general principles of the Bill. Where the subject matter of the Bill falls within the remit of more than one committee, one of these is designated as the lead committee, but the other committees may also consider the general principles of the Bill and report their views to the lead committee. If the Bill contains a provision which confers powers to make subordinate legislation, that provision must be referred to the Subordinate Legislation Committee which reports its views back to the lead committee[22].

The introduction of a Bill is roughly equivalent to the First Reading stage of a Bill in the UK Parliament but much more is required of the member in charge of a Bill in the Scottish Parliament by way of accompanying documents etc than is required in the UK Parliament. The intention of these requirements is to give the members of the lead committee and MSPs generally more information and to improve the quality and the acceptability of Acts of the Scottish Parliament.

Stage 1

First, the lead committee considers the general principles of the Bill, taking account of the views, if any, of other committees, and it also considers the Scottish Executive's policy memorandum. It then prepares a report for the Parliament. The

---

[18] This is also part of the pre-legislative scrutiny of the Bill. See p 55.
[19] Rule 9.3.3.
[20] Rule 9.3.4. For the Scottish Consolidated Fund and the Auditor General, see ch 8.
[21] For the Parliamentary Bureau, see ch 4.
[22] Rules 9.6.1, 9.6.2.

lead committee takes evidence, both oral and written, from a range of relevant witnesses, including individuals and interest groups. Other Committees may also take evidence and report to the lead committee. Ministers too may give evidence to the lead committee (or to other committees). The evidence taken at the Stage 1 inquiry can lead to quite significant amendments to Bills at Stage 2. For example, the Public Bodies and Public Appointments etc (Scotland) Bill proposed the abolition of the Ancient Monuments Board for Scotland and the Historic Buildings Council for Scotland without making provision for their replacement by any statutory body which could advise Ministers on aspects of Scotland's historic environment. As a result of evidence given to the lead committee and incorporated into its Stage 1 report, the Scottish Executive moved amendments to the Bill at Stage 2 to provide for the establishment of an Historic Environment Advisory Committee for Scotland.

The full Parliament considers the general principles of the Bill in the light of the lead committee's report. (At this stage it is open to any MSP to move that the Bill be referred back to the lead committee for a further report. If that motion is agreed to, the Parliament's consideration of the Bill is postponed until the further report has been presented to it.) The Parliament then decides, on a vote if necessary, whether or not the Bill's general principles are agreed to. If they are, the Bill proceeds to Stage 2; if not, the Bill falls[23]. The latter part of this stage is equivalent to the Second Reading stage in the UK Parliament.

Financial Resolution

Where a Bill contains provisions which introduce new expenditure or increase existing expenditure charged out of the Scottish Consolidated Fund or which impose or increase any tax or charge, there can be no proceedings after Stage 1 until the Parliament has, by resolution, agreed to this. Such a resolution can be moved only by a member of the Scottish Executive or a junior Minister[24].

Stage 2

The Bill is now referred back to the lead committee for detailed consideration. There must be a period of at least seven sitting days between the completion of Stage 1 and the beginning of Stage 2. The committee examines the Bill section by section[25] and considers amendments. Each section, whether amended or not, must be agreed to. It is open to any MSP to move an amendment to the Bill and participate in the debate on that amendment, but an MSP who is not a member of the committee may not vote on the amendment. It is possible for Stage 2 to be taken by a Committee of the Whole Parliament or by a committee which is not the lead committee.[26] At the end of Stage 2, if the Bill has been amended, the Clerk of the Parliament arranges for the amended Bill to be printed and published.

---

[23] Rules 9.6.3–9.6.7.
[24] Rule 9.12.
[25] Note that a Scottish Parliament Bill is divided into sections. A UK Parliament Bill is divided into clauses which become sections when the Bill becomes an Act of Parliament.
[26] Rule 9.7.

Stage 3

This stage is taken by the full Parliament and thus gives every MSP an opportunity to consider and vote on the Bill in its amended form. Nine sitting days must elapse between the completion of Stage 2 and the beginning of Stage 3 if the Bill has been amended at Stage 2, four sitting days if it has not been amended. At Stage 3, the Parliament must decide whether to pass the Bill. It is open to any MSP to give notice of an amendment to be taken at this stage and it is possible for the member in charge of the Bill to move that no more than half the total number of sections should be referred back to the committee for further Stage 2 consideration but such a reference back may happen only once. If there is a vote on the question of whether the Bill is passed, the result is valid only if the number of members voting is more than a quarter of the total number of seats in the Parliament, ie at least 33. Stage 3 is the equivalent of the Report and Third Reading stages in the UK Parliament.[27]

Subject to the possible four-week delay (referred to above[28]) and a reconsideration stage, the Bill is now ready to be presented to the Queen by the Presiding Officer for Royal Assent.

Reconsideration Stage

On occasion, it may be necessary for the Bill to be reconsidered by the Parliament. This will happen in the following circumstances:

- if one of the Law Officers has referred a question about legislative competence to the Judicial Committee of the Privy Council, and the Judicial Committee of the Privy Council has made a reference to the European Court of Justice for a preliminary ruling and neither of these references has been decided; or
- if the Judicial Committee of the Privy Council has decided that the Bill or any provision of it is outwith the legislative competence of the Parliament; or
- if an order has been made by a Secretary of State prohibiting the Presiding Officer from presenting the Bill for Royal Assent.[29]

The reconsideration stage is taken by the full Parliament and the only amendments which may be moved at this stage are amendments to resolve the problem. Once the amendments have been disposed of, the Parliament decides the question of whether to approve the Bill.[30]

Table 5.1, at the end of this chapter, shows how Executive Bills make their passage through the Parliament.

The Sewel Convention

A practice has developed since 1999 of the Scottish Parliament granting specific consent to the UK Parliament to legislate in devolved areas to ensure, for

---

[27] Rule 9.8.
[28] See p 55.
[29] For more information, see pp 55–56.
[30] Rule 9.9.

example, cross-border uniformity of legislation. To counter fears that the UK Parliament might choose to legislate in devolved areas without the consent of the Scottish Parliament, the junior Scottish Minister, Lord Sewel, who was in charge of the Scotland Bill during its passage through the House of Lords in 1998, stated that the UK Government expected that a convention would become established at Westminster that the UK Parliament would not normally legislate in devolved areas without the consent of the Scottish Parliament. This requirement for the consent of the Scottish Parliament has become known as the Sewel Convention and the consent is given by way of motions known as 'Sewel motions'. An early example of this convention in operation was in relation to the Food Standards Bill which established a UK Food Standards Agency. The Convention has been used rather more often than might have been expected and is criticised by some MSPs as a diminution of the Scottish Parliament's powers[31].

Committee Bills

Committee Bills are an innovation in the British law-making process and there is no equivalent procedure in the UK Parliament. The ability of committees of the Parliament to initiate legislation is in keeping with the spirit of giving them an opportunity to play a major part in the work of the Parliament. A proposal for a Committee Bill may be made either by a committee of the Parliament or by an individual MSP. If the proposal is made by an MSP, it is referred to the appropriate committee by the Parliamentary Bureau. (If a Committee Bill is introduced as a result of an MSP's proposal, it counts against the MSP's quota of two Member's Bills per session.) Prior to deciding whether to make a proposal, a committee may hold an inquiry into the need for the Bill. The proposal takes the form of a report to the Parliament setting out the committee's recommendations as to the provisions to be contained in the Bill, together with an explanation of the need for the Bill. If the Parliament agrees to the proposal, the convener of the committee may introduce the Bill unless a member of the Scottish Executive or a junior Scottish Minister has indicated that an Executive Bill is to be introduced to give effect to the proposal. A Committee Bill must go through the same three stages as for an Executive Bill, described above (with a reconsideration stage and a financial resolution if necessary), except that at Stage 1 it is referred immediately to the Parliament. A report by a lead committee on the Bill's general principles is not required as the committee initiating the Bill has already carried out all the preliminary work necessary[32].

Table 5.1 at the end of this chapter shows how Committee Bills make their passage through Parliament. At the end of the first four-year session of the Parliament, three Committee Bills had been passed: the Protection from Abuse Act 2001, the Scottish Parliamentary Standards Commissioner Act 2002, and the Commissioner for Children and Young People (Scotland) Act 2003.

Members' Bills

A Member's Bill is the equivalent of a Private Member's Bill in the UK Parliament. It is a Bill which is introduced by an MSP who is not a member of the

---

[31] For further information on the Sewel Convention see Ch 7 and also Winetrobe (2001) 6 SLPQ 286–292 and Page and Batey [2002] PL 501–523.

[32] Rule 9.15.

Scottish Executive. Such members are sometimes (inaccurately) referred to as backbenchers. Each member is entitled to introduce two Bills in any one session which gives a potential number of around two hundred in each four-year session. The procedures for Members' Bills are much more satisfactory than the procedures at Westminster which can literally be a bit of a lottery where prospects of progress depend very much on how high a place the MP concerned draws in the ballot for Private Members' Bills.

There are two options open to an MSP who is not a member of the Scottish Executive for the introduction of a Bill.

Option 1

The MSP submits to the Parliamentary Bureau a draft proposal for a Bill. The Parliamentary Bureau then refers the draft proposal to the relevant committee and the committee then decides whether to make the proposal as a Committee Bill (see Committee Bills above)[33]. Such a Bill is not technically a Member's Bill but it counts against the member's allocation of two per session.

Option 2

The MSP gives notice of a proposal for a Bill, setting out the proposed short title of the Bill and a brief explanation of its purpose, by lodging it with the clerks. The notice is then published in the Parliament's Business Bulletin for a period of one month. During that month the MSP must gather the support of at least eleven other MSPs to enable a Bill giving effect to the proposal to be introduced. If sufficient support is not gathered during that period, the proposal falls and a similar proposal may not be introduced by any MSP within six months[34]. A Member's Bill must pass through the three stages of a Bill described above, with a reconsideration stage and a financial resolution, if necessary.

Table 5.1 at the end of this chapter shows how a Bill proposed by a Member makes its way through the Parliament. At the end of the first session of the Parliament, eight Members' Bills had reached the statute book, including the Abolition of Poindings and Warrant Sales Act 2001, the Protection of Wild Mammals (Scotland) Act 2002 and the Dog Fouling (Scotland) Act 2003.

Private Bills

A Private Bill is a Bill which is introduced by an individual person, by a body corporate or by an unincorporated association of persons. The person who introduces such a Bill is known as 'the promoter'. The promoter is seeking particular powers or benefits which go beyond or are in conflict with the general law. Thus, it is important that anyone who objects to the proposal has an opportunity to state his or her objections. A local authority, for example, may need additional powers to acquire land to construct a ring road or an airport or a harbour and may acquire these powers by promoting a Private Bill[35]. An individual may promote a Private

---

[33] Rule 9.15.4.
[34] Rule 9.14.
[35] It should be noted that all Bills which are not Private Bills are Public Bills.

Bill in relation to his or her estate, property, status or style. Such Bills promoted by individuals (sometimes referred to as 'personal Bills') are likely to be fairly rare.

The procedures for private Bills are fairly complicated and only a brief outline is given here. Readers who wish more detail are referred to Chapter 9A of the Parliament's Standing Orders.

A Private Bill can be introduced into the Parliament on any sitting day by being lodged with the clerks and it must be signed by or on behalf of the promoter. Depending on the nature of the Bill, a wide range of accompanying documents may be required. The accompanying documents should include details of the advertisement of the promoter's intention and a statement as to where various relevant documents may be inspected. In the case of a so-called 'works Bill', maps, plans and sections of the works proposed to be authorised by the Bill are required.

After the Bill has been introduced, the Parliament establishes a Private Bill Committee to consider it. A Private Bill Committee must have no more than five members, none of whom should reside in or represent an area to be affected by the Bill. The members are expected to attend all the meetings of the committee. There is a 60-day 'objection period' during which objections may be lodged with the clerks either in writing or by email (later confirmed in writing).

A Private Bill goes through three stages:

- a Preliminary Stage at which the Private Bill Committee considers the general principles of the Bill and whether it should proceed as a private Bill. At the end of this stage, the Parliament takes a decision as to whether to agree those general principles and whether the Bill should proceed or not;
- a Consideration Stage at which the details of the Bill are considered by the Private Bill Committee. At this stage the promoter and objectors are invited to give evidence to the members and the Bill may be amended by the Committee in much the same way as at Stage 2 of a Public Bill; and
- a Final Stage at which the Parliament may further amend the Bill and then decide whether to pass or reject the Bill.

As with Public Bills, a Private Bill may have to go through a Reconsideration Stage[36]. At the end of the first session of the Scottish Parliament only one Private Bill had reached the statute book – the National Galleries of Scotland Act 2003. Private Bills which have not reached the statute book by the end of a four-year parliamentary session are carried over into the new parliamentary session. Table 5.2 at the end of this chapter shows how a Private Bill makes its way through the Parliament.

Emergency Bills

The process described above for Executive Bills has inbuilt delays of at least two weeks between Stages 1 and 2 and between Stages 2 and 3, if the Bill has been

---

[36] Rule 9A.5.

amended[37]. But there must be a procedure which allows the Scottish Executive to deal with emergencies. The SA 1998 allows for this and the Parliament's Standing Orders thus make special fast-track provisions for such situations[38].

Any member of the Scottish Executive or a junior Scottish Minister may move that a Bill introduced as an Executive Bill shall be treated as an Emergency Bill. If the Parliament agrees, the Bill is referred immediately to the Parliament for Stage 1 consideration without the necessity of a report on the Bill's general principles from a committee. Stage 2 is taken by a Committee of the whole Parliament. The requirement of minimum intervals between Stages 1 and 2 and between stages 2 and 3 is dispensed with and all stages of the Bill are normally taken on the day that the Parliament decides that the Bill is to be treated as an Emergency Bill. The first Bill passed by the Scottish Parliament – the Mental Health (Public Safety and Appeals) (Scotland) Bill 1999 – was treated as an Emergency Bill and passed through all stages and received Royal Assent within a fortnight.

Budget Bills

A Budget Bill is an Executive Bill, the purpose of which is to authorise sums to be paid out of the Scottish Consolidated Fund or to authorise sums received to be applied without being paid into that fund[39]. A Budget Bill can be introduced only by a member of the Scottish Executive and does not need to be accompanied by a Financial Memorandum, Explanatory Notes or a Policy Memorandum[40].

At Stage 1 a Budget Bill is referred immediately to the full Parliament for consideration of its principles and a decision as to whether these are agreed to. A report from a committee on general principles is not required and Stage 2 of the Bill is taken by the Finance Committee. The normal minimum intervals between stages do not apply, but Stage 3 is not to begin earlier than 20 days after introduction of the Bill. If Stage 3 is not completed before the expiry of 30 days after introduction, the Bill falls. Amendments to a Budget Bill may be moved only by a member of the Scottish Executive or a junior Scottish minister[41].

If a Budget Bill is dependent on the Parliament passing a tax-varying resolution[42] which would result in an increase of the basic rate of income tax for Scottish taxpayers and the Parliament rejects such a resolution, the Bill falls. However, if a Budget Bill falls or is rejected at any stage, a Bill in the same or similar terms can be introduced at any time thereafter[43].

Miscellaneous other Bills

The Scottish Parliament may also pass:

- Consolidation Bills the purpose of which is to restate existing law with or without amendments, to give effect to recommendations of the

---

[37] See pp 59–61.
[38] SA 1998, s 36(2); and r 9.21.
[39] For the Scottish Consolidated Fund, see Ch 8.
[40] Rule 9.16.2.
[41] Rules 9.16.3–9.16.6.
[42] Ie in accordance with SA 1998, s 73.
[43] Rules 9.16.7–9.16.8.

Scottish Law Commission or of the Scottish Law Commission and the (English) Law Commission jointly[44]. The first consolidation Bill – the Salmon and Freshwater Fisheries (Consolidation) (Scotland) Act 2003 – was passed at the end of the Parliament's first four-year session;

- Statute Law Repeals Bills the purpose of which is to repeal, in accordance with the Scottish Law Commission's recommendations, statute law which is out of date and no longer relevant[45];

- Statute Law Revision Bills the purpose of which is to revise statute law by repealing Acts which are no longer in force or have become unnecessary and re-enacting provisions of Acts of the Scottish Parliament or the UK Parliament which are otherwise spent[46].

CHALLENGES TO THE LEGISLATION

As mentioned above, Bills are subject to pre-legislative consideration and to further scrutiny after they have been passed to ensure that they do not stray beyond the Parliament's legislative competence. However, the courts have power even after legislation has been enacted to decide that an Act (or part of it) deals with matters outside the Parliament's legislative competence, and by so doing in effect strike down its legislation. As s 40(3) of the SA 1998 states that a court cannot make an order for suspension or reduction against the Parliament, it would appear that it could not as such 'cancel' an item of legislation made by the Parliament. However, if asked to do so, the court would be able to declare that an item of legislation is outside the Parliament's legislative competence. As s 29(1) of the SA 1998 states that an Act of the Scottish Parliament is not law so far as any provision of it is outside the legislative competence of the Parliament, the effect of such a declaration would be to make the Act concerned, or certain of its provisions, null and void from the time of enactment. In practice, rather than leave it to the courts to make such a declaration, it is more likely that if an item of legislation were declared to be outside the Parliament's legislative competence, the Parliament would itself amend the legislation accordingly. If it did not, the UK Parliament or Ministers would be able to make the necessary amendment anyway.

Challenges to the Parliament's legislation are considered in more detail in Chapter 7.

SUBORDINATE LEGISLATION MADE BY SCOTTISH MINISTERS

Much UK legislation is enacted not as primary legislation which must pass through the full Parliamentary procedure, but as subordinate legislation usually in the form of a statutory instrument. Such legislation consists of either an order made by a Minister or an Order in Council made by the Queen on the advice of her Ministers. Some existing powers to make subordinate legislation under Acts of the UK Parliament were transferred to the Scottish Ministers when the Scottish Parliament and Executive were first established in 1999. In addition, Acts of the Scottish Parliament may confer powers on Scottish Ministers to make subordinate legis-

---

[44] Rule 9.18.
[45] Rule 9.19. Such laws are known as 'spent enactments'.
[46] Rule 9.20.

lation in any area in which the Scottish Parliament has legislative competence[47]. The SA 1998 places some restrictions on the power to make subordinate legislation under an Act of the Scottish Parliament. For example, serious criminal offences cannot be created by such legislation[48].

A piece of subordinate legislation made under an Act of the Scottish Parliament is called a Scottish Statutory Instrument (SSI).

Procedures for making subordinate legislation

The SA 1998 does not lay down procedures for the making of subordinate legislation within devolved areas. Instead, the procedures are set out in a statutory instrument made under the SA 1998[49]. Provisions for scrutiny of Scottish Statutory Instruments are set out in the Parliament's Standing Orders[50]. The procedures are largely based on the Westminster model.

As at Westminster, most instruments are subject to either a negative procedure (subject to annulment) or an affirmative procedure (requiring approval by resolution). Under the negative procedure, the instrument becomes law unless the Parliament resolves that nothing further is to be done under the instrument, ie to annul the instrument. Under the affirmative procedure, the Parliament must resolve to approve the instrument for it to become law. The affirmative procedure is thus the stronger form of scrutiny. The parent Act[51] lays down which procedure is to be used and, in some cases, the parent Act may provide that the instrument is to be made without being subject to either affirmative or negative procedure, or even without requiring it to be laid before Parliament.

Scrutiny by committees

The Scottish Parliament has a committee called the Subordinate Legislation Committee[52], similar to the Joint Committee on Statutory Instruments at Westminster, which scrutinises the technical aspects of every piece of subordinate legislation which is laid before the Parliament. The Subordinate Legislation Committee also has the power to scrutinise provisions in Bills which confer powers on Scottish Ministers to make subordinate legislation. Subordinate legislation is also scrutinised by at least one subject committee of the Scottish Parliament or by the Parliament as a whole, a procedure which has no direct Westminster parallel.

An instrument or draft instrument (ie an actual or a proposed piece of subordinate legislation) is said to be laid before the Parliament if a copy of it is lodged with the clerks during office hours. Once laid, the clerks refer the instrument to the Subordinate Legislation Committee and to the lead committee, ie the subject

---

[47] SA 1998, ss 53, 54, 112.

[48] SA 1998, s 113(10).

[49] Scotland Act 1998 (Transitory and Transitional Provisions) (Statutory Instruments) Order 1999, SI 1999/1096.

[50] The rules for making subordinate legislation are contained in Ch 10 of the Parliament's Standing Orders.

[51] The parent Act is the Act which empowers Ministers to make subordinate legislation relating to that Act.

[52] The Subordinate Legislation Committee is one of the mandatory committees of the Scottish Parliament, ie the Parliament *must* establish such a committee. See Ch 4.

committee within whose remit the subject matter of the instrument falls, unless the Parliament has decided that the instrument should be considered by the full Parliament. If the subject matter falls within the remit of more than one subject committee, one of the committees is designated as the lead committee and the instrument is sent to the other committee(s) as well which may make recommendations to the lead committee[53].

The remit of the Subordinate Legislation Committee is to decide whether the attention of the Parliament should be drawn to the instrument on the following grounds[54]:

- it imposes a charge on the Scottish Consolidated Fund[55] or contains provisions requiring payments to be made to various bodies;
- it is made under an Act (the parent Act) which specifically excludes challenge in the courts;
- it appears to have retrospective effect although the parent Act does not confer the authority to do so;
- there appears to be unjustifiable delay in publishing the instrument or in laying it before the Parliament;
- there appears to be a doubt as to whether it is *intra vires*;
- it raises a devolution issue;
- it has been made by what appears to be an unusual or unexpected use of the powers conferred by the parent Act;
- for any special reason its form or meaning could be clearer;
- its drafting appears to be defective;

or on any other ground which does not impinge on its substance or the policy behind it. The Subordinate Legislation Committee must report its decision with its reasons to the Parliament and to the lead committee within 20 days of the laying of the instrument[56].

Motion for annulment (negative procedure)

The negative procedure is a weaker form of control of subordinate legislation because the instrument becomes (or remains) law after a certain period if no MSP successfully moves its annulment.

No later than 40 days after the instrument has been laid, any MSP (whether or not a member of the lead committee) can propose to the lead committee that nothing further should be done under the instrument. The lead committee is allowed to have a debate of no more than 90 minutes on this proposal and the MSP who has made that proposal, along with the Minister in charge of the instrument, may participate in the debate but not vote on the proposal.

The lead committee then reports to the Parliament, within 40 days of the instrument being laid, with its recommendations. If the lead committee recommends that no further action should be taken, i e that the instrument should not be made,

---

[53] Rules 10.1, 10.2.
[54] Rule 10.3.
[55] For the Scottish Consolidated Fund, see Ch 8.
[56] Rule 10.3.

a very limited debate takes place, a vote is taken if necessary and if the motion to annul is agreed to the Minister is then required to annul the instrument[57].

Motion for approval (affirmative procedure)

The affirmative procedure is a stronger form of control of subordinate legislation because the instrument cannot become (or remain) law unless it has been approved by the Parliament. The lead committee must decide whether to recommend to the Parliament that an affirmative instrument should be approved. Any member of the Scottish Executive or a junior Minister, even if not a member of the lead committee, may propose to the lead committee that it should recommend approval. As with the negative procedure, that member (if not a member of the committee) and the Minister in charge of the instrument may participate in the 90-minute debate but may not vote. The lead committee must make its recommendation to the Parliament within 40 days of its being laid. If approval is recommended, only very limited debate is allowed and if the motion to approve is agreed to, after a vote if necessary, the instrument becomes (or remains) law[58].

Instruments which do not require the Parliament's approval

Some Acts of the Scottish Parliament may provide that an instrument laid before the Parliament may be made without the Parliament's approval. Such instruments should not be contentious, but the Parliament's Standing Orders do allow MSPs to have some control over them. The procedure is very similar to the negative procedure described above. No later than 40 days after the instrument has been laid, any MSP may propose to the lead committee that the committee should recommend to the Parliament that the instrument be not made. That MSP and the Minister in charge of the instrument are entitled to participate in the 90-minute debate but may not vote if they are not members of the lead committee. If the lead committee recommends to the Parliament that the instrument should not be made, the procedure is as described above[59].

Although the Scottish Ministers normally make subordinate legislation only in areas in which the Parliament has legislative competence, some possibilities exist for Scottish Ministers to make subordinate legislation in areas where the Parliament itself has not been given powers to legislate. The SA 1998 contains a power allowing for functions exercisable by a UK Minister to be transferred, by Order in Council, to Scottish Ministers (or to be exercised concurrently by both UK and Scottish Ministers), in so far as the functions concerned relate to Scotland[60]. This allows Scottish Ministers to make subordinate legislation in relation to matters concerning Scotland, but in which legislative power has not been devolved to the Parliament. (However, such a transfer can take place only with the approval of the Scottish Parliament, and also both Houses of the UK Parliament[61].) The SA 1998 also includes specific provision allowing an Order in

---

[57] Rule 10.4.
[58] Rule 10.6.
[59] Rule 10.5.
[60] SA 1998, s 63. There is a parallel provision allowing for the transfer of functions from Scottish Ministers to UK Ministers in s 108.
[61] SA 1998, Sch 7, para 2.

Council to be made giving powers to Scottish Ministers to make subordinate legislation concerning the regulation of the Tweed and Esk fisheries[62].

THE LEGISLATIVE LOAD

At the beginning of the first session of the Parliament, the First Minister announced a legislative programme of eight Executive Bills for the first year of the Parliament. At the end of December 1999, when the Parliament had been in existence for six months, only one Act of the Scottish Parliament (asp) had reached the statute book – the Mental Health (Public Safety and Appeals) (Scotland) Act 1999 – and that arose from an Emergency Bill. Three other Executive Bills and one Member's Bill were in progress while a further six Member's Bills were at the proposal stage. No Committee Bills had been introduced by that date. In contrast, the Parliament had made around two hundred Scottish Statutory Instruments (SSIs) within the same period.

At the close of the Parliament's first term on 31 March 2003, the Parliament had passed 62 Acts. Of these, fifty had been introduced as Executive Bills, three as Committee Bills, eight as Members' Bills and one as a Private Bill. Very few of these would have reached the statute book if there had not been a Scottish Parliament as the UK Parliament did not make much time available for Scottish Bills. In addition to the 62 Acts of the Scottish Parliament, nearly two thousand Scottish Statutory Instruments had been made.

UK SUBORDINATE LEGISLATION AND THE SCOTTISH PARLIAMENT AND MINISTERS

The SA 1998 also gives the Parliament and Scottish Ministers a degree of involvement in respect of other matters in which legislative competence has not been devolved to the Parliament[63]. The powers include those listed below, and can be grouped into three types.

First, certain provisions which enable subordinate legislation to be made by Order in Council can be exercised only with the approval of the Parliament, as follows (in all but the first case the approval of both Houses of the UK Parliament is also required):

- the power to disqualify specified public office-holders from becoming an MSP[64];
- the power to modify the list of reserved matters on which the Parliament cannot legislate[65];
- the power to transfer additional functions from UK Ministers to Scottish Ministers[66];
- the power to make payment to opposition political parties to assist MSPs in carrying out their duties[67];

---

[62] SA 1998, s 111.
[63] SA 1998, Sch 7.
[64] SA 1998, s 15.
[65] SA 1998, s 30.
[66] SA 1998, s 63.
[67] SA 1998, s 97.

- the redistribution of functions exercisable by Scottish Ministers in whole or in part to UK Ministers[68].

Second, there are certain matters in respect of which the Scottish Parliament can annul proposals for UK subordinate legislation, as follows:

- the transfer of property and liabilities from UK Ministers to Scottish Ministers or the Lord Advocate (and vice versa)[69];
- specifying functions which a UK Minister can arrange by agreement to be carried out by a Scottish Minister or the Lord Advocate (and vice versa)[70];
- an order made by the Scottish Minister setting the level of the deposit (caution) which has to be lodged by a person seeking the disqualification of an MSP[71];
- the adaptation of the functions of a 'cross-border public authority'[72] and the transfer of the property and liabilities of such bodies (unless, in these cases, the Parliament (and the UK Parliament) has previously approved the subordinate legislation in question)[73].

(If the UK subordinate legislation in the above cases, except in the case of setting the level of caution, changes the text of an Act of Parliament, the Scottish Parliament, and both Houses of the UK Parliament, have to approve the proposal by a positive vote in support of it.)

Third, there are certain cases in which the Scottish Ministers have to be consulted before subordinate legislation is made by the relevant UK authority, including the following:

- an order made by the UK Treasury designating those government receipts which are to be payable into the Scottish Consolidated Fund – the Treasury is required to consult with the Scottish Ministers before making such designation[74];
- the exercise of certain powers by UK Ministers over cross-border public authorities – in some circumstances the UK Minister must consult the Scottish Ministers before exercising functions in relation to a cross-border public authority[75];
- subordinate legislation transferring certain functions to Scottish Ministers where that modifies certain obligations under international or EU law – the Scottish Ministers must be consulted before any such legislation is made[76].

The legislative process of the Scottish Parliament is illustrated by diagrams in Tables 5.1 and 5.2.

---

[68] SA 1998, s 108.
[69] SA 1998, s 109.
[70] SA 1998, s 93.
[71] SA 1998, s 18.
[72] See ch 9 on cross-border public authorities.
[73] SA 1998, ss 89 and 90.
[74] SA 1998, s 64.
[75] SA 1998, s 88; and see ch 9.
[76] SA 1998, s 106.

Table 5.1 Stages in the passage of a Public Bill

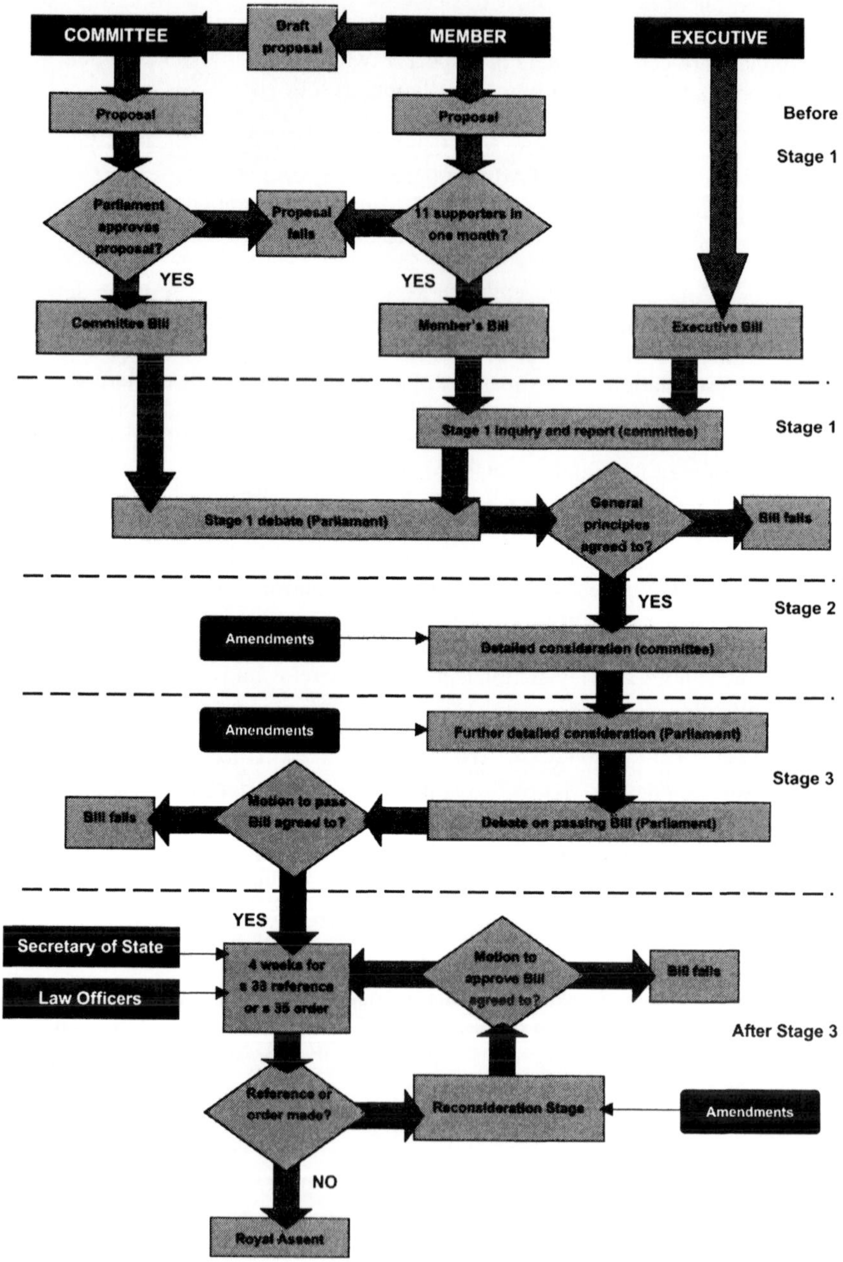

Table 5.2   Private Bill process

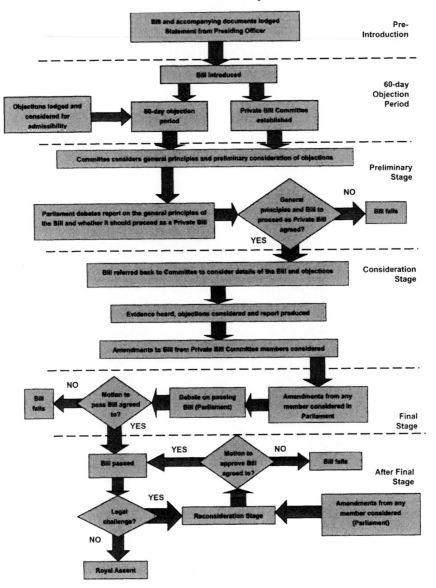

6 THE SCOTTISH GOVERNMENT

INTRODUCTION

The establishment of a Scottish Parliament has given Scotland not only a legislature, but also a government which may take executive action over the whole range of devolved functions. The Scotland Act 1998 (SA 1998) describes it as the Scottish Administration but it is generally known as the Scottish Executive. It is based on the Westminster model of parliamentary government. The Ministers are drawn from the ranks of the MSPs and are accountable to them. In the UK Government the rules relating to the appointment of the Prime Minister and the other Ministers of the UK Parliament are largely unwritten and are based on convention. The equivalent rules for the appointment of the First Minister and the other Ministers of the Scottish Parliament are statutory and are to be found in Part II of the SA 1998.

The Scottish Executive consists of the First Minister, Scottish Ministers and the Scottish Law Officers, ie the Lord Advocate and the Solicitor General for Scotland[1]. No person who holds Ministerial office in the UK Government is allowed to be appointed as a Minister in the Scottish Administration. Thus, anyone who is elected to the Scottish Parliament and who already holds Ministerial office in Her Majesty's Government in any of the UK Departments of State has to give that office up if he or she is to become a Scottish Minister. This rule applies also to the First Minister. Thus, Donald Dewar, who was Secretary of State for Scotland prior to the first general election to the Scottish Parliament in 1999, resigned from that office in order to be appointed as a member of the Scottish Executive and First Minister.

THE FIRST MINISTER

The First Minister is the equivalent of the Prime Minister. He or she is appointed by the Queen from among the Members of the Scottish Parliament within 28 days of a general election and holds office 'at Her Majesty's pleasure'[2]. Theoretically this means that the First Minister could be dismissed by the Queen for good reason or for none. In practice, the First Minister holds office as long as he or she can command the support of the majority of the MSPs. Therefore, the person appointed as First Minister is normally the leader of the party able to command the majority support of the MSPs. Since the electoral system to the Scottish Parliament has an element of proportional representation in it, it is unlikely that any one single party will win a clear majority of the seats. In the first elections the Labour Party won 56 of the 129 seats and thus did not have a clear majority. A coalition agreement was reached with the Liberal Democrats[3] and, as part of the

---

[1] SA 1998, s 44.

[2] SA 1998, s 45(1).

[3] The terms of the coalition agreement are to be found in *Partnership for Scotland: An Agreement for the First Scottish Parliament* (May 1999).

agreement, the leader of the Labour Party, Donald Dewar, emerged as the favoured candidate for the post of First Minister with the Leader of the Liberal Democrats, Jim Wallace, as his deputy. In the elections of 2003, the Labour Party won 50 seats and were still the largest party. Again they formed a coalition with the Liberal Democrats (who had won 17 seats) and Jack McConnell, the leader of the Labour Party became First Minister with Jim Wallace again as his deputy[4].

The Parliament's Standing Orders set out the procedure for the nomination of an MSP for appointment as First Minister[5]. Any member may nominate a candidate by submitting a nomination to the Clerk of the Parliament in writing. To be valid, the nomination must be seconded by another MSP. The candidates must have taken the oath of allegiance before voting takes place. An electronic voting system is normally used, but if the Presiding Officer thinks that that system cannot be used for any reason or that it has produced an unreliable result, the vote may be taken by ballot or by roll call or any other method. The names of the candidates are read out by the Presiding Officer and then there is a vote or a series of votes until one single candidate emerges who has the support of the majority of MSPs voting[6]. The quorum for this vote is 25 per cent plus one which seems very low for such an important decision. Following the selection of the candidate by the Parliament, the Presiding Officer recommends that candidate to the Queen for appointment and the Queen appoints the candidate.

If the office of First Minister is vacant, or he or she is for any reason, such as prolonged illness, unable to act, his or her functions are exercisable by another MSP designated by the Presiding Officer[7]. No doubt the Presiding Officer consults the party leaders privately to try to identify a Member who would be generally acceptable. When the First Minister, Donald Dewar, became ill in 2000, the Deputy First Minister, Jim Wallace, deputised as he did in the immediate period after Donald Dewar's death. The First Minister may resign at any time and must do so if the Scottish Executive loses the confidence of the Scottish Parliament[8]. A new First Minister must be nominated for appointment within 28 days of the post becoming vacant, otherwise an extraordinary general election must be held[9].

THE FUNCTIONS OF THE FIRST MINISTER

The First Minister is, in many ways, the Scottish Prime Minister. He or she is normally the leader of the party with the largest number of seats in the Scottish Parliament, the Leader of the Scottish Executive and the chief channel of communication with the UK Prime Minister.

Certain powers of appointment are specifically conferred on the First Minister by the SA 1998 which, in the case of the UK Prime Minister, are largely conventional. The First Minister, with the agreement of the Parliament, recommends names to the Queen for appointment as Ministers, junior Ministers, the Law

---

[4] The terms of the second coalition agreement are to be found in a *Partnership for a Better Scotland* (May 2003).

[5] The rules relating to the nomination of the First Minister and the appointment of members of the Scottish Executive are contained in Ch 4 of the Parliament's Standing Orders.

[6] The procedures relating to the selection of the First Minister are to be found in rule 11.10 of the Parliament's Standing Orders.

[7] SA 1998, s 45(4).

[8] SA 1998, s 45(2).

[9] See ch 3, pp 24–25.

Officers[10]. Ministers and junior Ministers may be removed from office by the First Minister. In the case of the Law Officers, the First Minister may, with the agreement of the Parliament, recommend their removal to the Queen[11]. The Act allows for executive functions to be conferred on the First Minister alone and the doctrine of collective responsibility does not apply to his or her acts or omissions[12].

The crucial difference between the Scottish First Minister and the UK Prime Minister is that the former will almost always be the head of a coalition government, whereas the UK Prime Minister will normally have a working majority – at least as long as the first past the post system of voting is retained for elections to Westminster. Coalition with another political grouping inevitably constrains the freedom of action of the First Minister. In the allocation of portfolios to Ministers, he or she has to negotiate with the Leader of the smaller party or parties in the coalition as to how many Ministerial posts each party will have. The Labour–Liberal Democrat coalition which emerged after the first elections in May 1999 allocated two Ministerial posts and two junior Ministerial posts to the Liberal Democrats. In 2003 the coalition agreement gave the Liberal Democrats three ministerial posts and three junior Ministerial posts. The UK Prime Minister does not normally have this constraint in the allocation of portfolios. The same process of inter-party negotiation applies in the policies to be adopted, the prioritisation of Bills, the allocation of convenerships of committees and many other aspects of the business of government[13].

Nevertheless, the office of First Minister is a very powerful one. By presiding at Cabinet meetings, and setting its agenda to a large extent, the First Minister can control discussion and the process of decision making. He or she is expected to make major policy statements and intervene in the pressing issues of the day, such as Scottish industrial closures. The press and other media see the First Minister as Scotland's Prime Minister and give him or her enormous public exposure.

The appointment and removal of judges

The appointment and removal of judges is also largely within the First Minister's powers[14]. The two most senior judges in Scotland are the Lord President of the Court of Session and the Lord Justice-Clerk. The Prime Minister recommends the names of appropriate persons to the Queen, but he cannot recommend anyone for appointment who has not first been nominated by the First Minister. The First Minister also recommends to the Queen the names of persons for appointment as the other judges of the Court of Session, sheriffs principal and sheriffs, but only after consultation with the Lord President.

In practice, until fairly recently, it has been the Lord Advocate[15] who selects candidates for appointment as judges and sheriffs and recommends them to the First Minister. In February 2000, amidst some controversy, the first Lord Advocate in the new Scottish Parliament, Lord Hardie, recommended himself to the First Minister for appointment as a Court of Session judge. He was duly appointed and the Solicitor General, Colin Boyd, was promoted to fill the vacancy.

---

[10] SA 1998, ss 47–49.
[11] SA 1998, s 48
[12] SA 1998, s 52(5)(a).
[13] See *Partnership for a Better Scotland* (May 2003).
[14] SA 1998, s 95.
[15] For more information on the Lord Advocate, see p 78.

Giving the power of appointment of judges to the First Minister, who is a party politician, on the recommendation of the Lord Advocate who is also a member of the Scottish Executive, has been criticised as undermining the independence of the judiciary and contributed to the decision to dispense with temporary sheriffs and replace them with part-time sheriffs[16]. In an attempt to bring more transparency and independence to the appointment of members of the judiciary, the Scottish Executive issued a consultation paper on the possibility of a judicial appointments commission in the spring of 2000[17]. The responses to the consultation paper indicated substantial support for such a body and in 2001 the Justice Minister announced the establishment of the Judicial Appointments Board for Scotland. The Board has in membership five legal members and five lay members, the latter including the chairman. The remit of the Board is to provide the First Minister with a list of candidates recommended for appointment as judge of the Court of Session, sheriff principal, sheriff and part-time sheriff. Such recommendations are to be made on merit, but, in addition, the Board has to consider ways of making the judiciary as representative as possible of the communities which they serve. All vacancies are publicly advertised and no candidate is recommended for appointment without being interviewed.

The power to remove a judge of the Court of Session is even more controversial and provoked a great deal of debate during the passage of the SA 1998 through the House of Lords. Prior to the establishment of the Scottish Parliament, there was no power to remove such a judge from office in Scotland. The position in England is different: a judge may be removed from office following an address from the House of Commons and the House of Lords to the Queen. The Scotland Bill as originally drafted would have allowed the First Minister to recommend to the Queen the removal of a Court of Session judge and the Chairman of the Scottish Land Court following a resolution of the Parliament which was supported by at least two-thirds of the total number of MSPs. These provisions were amended by the House of Lords to build in a further stage to protect the independence of the judges. The procedure is presently governed by a transitional Order but is eventually to be governed by an Act of the Scottish Parliament.

The position now is that if there is any question of a judge of the Court of Session or the Chairman of the Scottish Land Court being unfit for office through inability, neglect of duty or misbehaviour, the First Minister may set up a tribunal of at least three persons, chaired by a member of the Judicial Committee of the Privy Council, to investigate and report on the matter. The First Minister must set up such a tribunal if requested to do so by the Lord President of the Court of Session and may do so in other circumstances if it is considered to be necessary. If the tribunal reports, in writing and with reasons, that the judge is unfit for office for one of the reasons given above, the First Minister is to move a resolution before the Parliament that a recommendation should be made to the Queen that the judge should be removed from office. The First Minister must obtain the approval of the Parliament, but there is now no requirement of a special majority. If the judge to be removed from office is either the Lord President or the Lord Justice-Clerk, the First Minister must consult the Prime Minister. The lesser penalty of suspension may be imposed.

---

[16] *Starrs and Chalmers v Ruxton* 2000 SLT 42, and ch 10.

[17] *Judicial Appointments: An Inclusive Approach* (2000).

SCOTTISH MINISTERS

The First Minister appoints a team of Scottish Ministers. Each Minister must be a Member of the Scottish Parliament. Ministers are appointed with the Queen's approval, but the First Minister must first seek the agreement of the Parliament to the nominations before submitting names to the Queen[18]. This is different from the procedure at Westminster where the Prime Minister can recommend to the Queen the appointment of whomsoever he wishes to Ministerial office, subject of course to political considerations, without having to secure the agreement of Parliament. Standing Orders allow the First Minister to seek the Scottish Parliament's approval for the appointment of Scottish Ministers either individually or *en bloc*. The Parliament is able to reject, but not to substitute the names of particular individuals in the First Minister's list. A simple majority of those voting is sufficient to secure Parliament's agreement and again the quorum is 25 per cent plus one[19]. The allocation of portfolios to Ministers is a decision for the First Minister alone subject to negotiation with the coalition partner(s), if any, and is not included in the motion seeking the Parliament's approval to appointment.

Scottish Ministers, like the First Minister, hold office at Her Majesty's pleasure. They may be removed from office by the First Minister and must resign if they lose the confidence of the Parliament[20]. The Presiding Officer notifies the Parliament of any resignation made by a member of the Scottish Executive. Ministers cease to hold office if they become disqualified to be MSPs for any reason (other than the calling of an election) such as bankruptcy or insanity.

In the UK Parliament, whose members are elected under the first past the post system, it is usual for one party to have an outright majority. Thus, UK ministers are normally MPs from one single political party, the party of government. In the Scottish Parliament some of whose members are elected under the regional list system discussed above,[21] coalition government is the norm and Scottish Ministers are appointed from the MSPs of the parties forming the coalition. The number of Ministers in the UK Cabinet is around 22. The number of Scottish Ministers appointed to the first Scottish Executive was ten. Following the election in 2003, the First Minister again appointed ten Ministers to his Cabinet, but two of these were appointed at the rank and salary of junior Ministers.

In addition to the oath of allegiance to the Queen which all members of the Scottish Parliament must take on election, members of the Scottish Executive must take the official oath as laid down in the Promissory Oaths Act 1868, in the following terms: 'I do swear that I will well and truly serve Her Majesty Queen Elizabeth in the office of Scottish Minister'.

THE SCOTTISH LAW OFFICERS

There are two Scottish Law Officers, namely the Lord Advocate and his or her deputy, the Solicitor General, who act as the senior legal advisers to the Scottish Executive and are themselves members of the Scottish Executive. In other words,

---

[18] SA 1998, s 47(2).

[19] The procedures relating to the appointment of Scottish Ministers are found in r 4.6 of the Parliament's Standing Orders.

[20] SA 1998, s 47(3).

[21] See ch 3.

they are political appointments. The Lord Advocate is also the head of the systems of criminal prosecution and investigation of deaths in Scotland and must act independently in those capacities.

Unlike the rest of the Scottish Ministers, they do not have to be Members of the Scottish Parliament and neither the first two Lords Advocate nor the first three Solicitors General were elected members of the Scottish Parliament. (It is quite possible that they may not even be members of a political party). The reason for this is that they have to be legally qualified and it may not be possible to find two MSPs who have the appropriate legal qualifications. They do, however, have to have the approval of Parliament before they can be appointed[22] and the same procedure as that used for the appointment of Scottish Ministers is used for securing the agreement of Parliament[23]. If they are not Members of the Parliament, they can still participate in Parliamentary proceedings but they may not vote[24]. They are able to participate in debates and answer questions, attend sessions of Committees, and steer through Parliament any Bills or secondary legislation for which they have responsibility. However, if asked any question in Parliament or asked to produce any document by the Parliament which relates to the operation of the system of criminal prosecution in a particular case, they may decline to do so on the grounds that it might prejudice criminal proceedings in that case or would otherwise be contrary to the public interest.

The First Minister, having obtained the agreement of the Parliament to their nominations, recommends the appointments to the Queen. They may resign at any time and must do so if the Scottish Executive loses the confidence of the Parliament. However, if the Lord Advocate has to resign as a result of a vote of no confidence in the Scottish Executive, he is deemed to remain in office as head of the systems of criminal prosecution and investigation of deaths in Scotland until a successor is appointed[25].

This is one of a number of provisions in the SA 1998 designed to safeguard the independence of the Scottish Law Officers. In addition, it is outwith the legislative competence of the Scottish Parliament to attempt to pass an Act which contains a provision which would remove the Lord Advocate from his position as head of the systems of criminal prosecution and investigation of deaths in Scotland[26]. Any decisions taken by him in either of those capacities must be taken by him independently.

However, the Lord Advocate is a member of the Scottish Executive and thus originally had a seat in the Scottish Cabinet. This came in for a certain amount of criticism from one of Scotland's most senior judges, Lord McCluskey, who argued that the Lord Advocate's membership of the Cabinet undermined judicial independence[27]. As a result of this criticism, the Lord Advocate gave up his right to vote in the Cabinet in October 2000 but still remains a member of the Scottish Executive.

---

[22] SA 1998, s 48.

[23] The procedures relating to the appointment, removal and parliamentary participation of the Law Officers are contained in rr 4.3–4.5 of the Parliament's Standing Orders.

[24] SA 1998, s 27.

[25] SA 1998, s 48(3).

[26] SA 1998, s 29(2)(e).

[27] See *The Herald*, 27 December 1999.

JUNIOR SCOTTISH MINISTERS

The First Minister may also appoint junior Scottish Ministers[28]. They are not technically members of the Scottish Executive as defined in the SA 1998, s 44 although they are considered as such. Section 49 of the SA 1998 which deals with their appointment does not set any limit to their number. In the UK Government there is a statutory limit. Not more than 95 members of the House of Commons may hold Ministerial office. The purpose of this (in theory at least) is to prevent the Executive from dominating Parliament. Political considerations and public opinion no doubt work together to ensure that a reasonable limit is set in the Scottish Parliament and in the first Parliament the number of junior Ministers appointed was ten. In the Parliament elected in 2003, seven junior Ministers were appointed. Junior Scottish Ministers are appointed in the same way as Scottish Ministers. With the agreement of the Parliament, the First Minister recommends their appointment to the Queen. They, too, hold office at Her Majesty's pleasure, may be removed from office by the First Minister, may resign at any time, and must do so if the Scottish Executive loses the confidence of the Scottish Parliament.

MINISTERIAL PARLIAMENTARY AIDES

A small number of MSPs may be appointed as Ministerial Parliamentary Aides. As the title suggests, they assist Cabinet Ministers in the discharge of their parliamentary duties. These are very junior posts and attract no additional financial allowance. They are roughly equivalent to Parliamentary Private Secretaries in the UK Government.

MOTIONS OF NO CONFIDENCE

It is a convention of the UK constitution that the Prime Minister and his Ministers resign if they lose a motion of no confidence. The SA 1998 puts this into statutory form. Sections 45(2), 47(3)(c), 48(2) and 49(4)(c) require the resignation of the First Minister, the Scottish Ministers, the Law Officers and junior Ministers respectively if Parliament resolves that the Scottish Executive no longer enjoys the confidence of the Parliament. If the Parliament subsequently fails to nominate a successor as First Minister, an extraordinary general election has to be called[29].

Any MSP is able to move a motion of no confidence in the Scottish Executive. The motion must be supported by at least 25 other MSPs in order to be included in the business programme of the Parliament. Normally, at least two days' notice of a motion of no confidence should be given, but the Parliamentary Bureau may decide that a shorter period is appropriate[30]. Such a motion requires a simple majority of those voting (subject to a quorum) for approval. The Parliament is also able to consider a motion of no confidence in a named Minister. This would not automatically lead to the resignation of the Minister as the SA 1998 does not

---

[28] SA 1998, s 49.

[29] See ch 3, pp 24–25.

[30] The procedures relating to motions of no confidence are found in r 8.12 of the Parliament's Standing Orders.

require this. However, the position of that Minister might become untenable after losing the confidence of the Parliament, and the First Minister might ask the Minister to resign.

THE CIVIL SERVICE

The Scottish Ministers may appoint such staff as they consider appropriate. These staff are in the Home Civil Service, as are staff serving in other departments of the Scottish Executive, including the Lord Advocate's Department[31]. The holders of various offices such as the Registrar General of Births, Deaths and Marriages for Scotland and the Keepers of the Records and Registers of Scotland are also in the Home Civil Service as are their staff. The UK Government considers that maintaining a unified Home Civil Service is essential for the preservation of the Union. It also preserves a career structure in the UK for Civil Servants and ensures that their terms and conditions of service are appropriately protected. Responsibility for the management of that staff ultimately remains with the Minister for the Civil Service (ie the Prime Minister), but in practice responsibility for the day-to-day management of staff is delegated to the Scottish Ministers as happens for UK Government departments.

The officers in the Scottish Executive are divided into six major departments. These are:

- the Scottish Executive Development Department which has responsibility for local government, social inclusion, housing, transport, planning, building control and European Structural Funds;
- the Scottish Executive Education Department which has responsibility for primary and secondary education and for the arts, cultural and built heritage and architectural policy, sport and Gaelic;
- the Scottish Executive Health Department which has responsibility for all aspects of the NHS and health generally in Scotland;
- the Scottish Executive Enterprise and Lifelong Learning Department which has responsibility for business and industry, further and higher education and lifelong learning;
- the Scottish Executive Justice Department which has responsibility for the police and fire services, Scottish courts administration, criminal justice, social work, legal aid and electoral procedures; and
- the Scottish Executive Environment and Rural Affairs Department which has responsibility for agriculture, the environment and fisheries.

There are also the Executive Secretariat, Corporate Services and the Finance and Central Services Department.

MINISTERIAL FUNCTIONS

Ministers of the UK Government exercise various powers most of which are conferred on them by an Act of Parliament. A few derive from the common law

---

[31] SA 1998, s 51.

and are called prerogative powers. As the Scottish Parliament began to pass its own Acts, powers were conferred by these Acts on Scottish Ministers. However, the SA 1998 contains a section which transferred existing prerogative and executive functions relating to devolved matters virtually in their entirety from UK Ministers to Scottish Ministers[32]. This was a sensible provision for the early days of the Scottish Parliament. Many of the early decisions taken by the Scottish Executive derived from powers conferred by an Act of the UK Parliament on a Secretary of State, usually the Secretary of State for Scotland. This section enabled the Scottish Ministers to take over immediately without requiring any other piece of empowering legislation.

As the Scottish Parliament started to enact its own legislation, s 52 of the SA 1998 enabled functions to be conferred directly on the First Minister, the Lord Advocate and the Scottish Ministers by Acts of the Scottish Parliament or by subordinate legislation. In the UK Parliament the duties of Secretaries of State are, in theory, interchangeable and this theory is continued into the Scottish Parliament with the provision that statutory functions may be exercised by any member of the Scottish Executive. The acts and omissions of any of them (other than the specific functions conferred on the First Minister or the Lord Advocate) are to be treated as the acts and omissions of each of them. This puts into statutory form the doctrine of collective responsibility.

There are some exceptions to the general rule about the transfer of powers from the UK Ministers to the Scottish Ministers where it makes sense for a UK Minister to share powers with Scottish Ministers – for example, the provision of grants or loans for transport infrastructure, the promotion of exports and the funding of scientific research[33]. UK Ministers also retain the power to make regulations for Scotland in order to implement European Community obligations and Scottish Ministers have no power to make subordinate legislation or to do any act which is incompatible with EC law or with rights under the European Convention on Human Rights[34].

COLLECTIVE RESPONSIBILITY

The acceptance of the constitutional doctrine of collective responsibility forms part of the coalition agreement between the Labour Party and the Liberal Democrats[35]. The partners in the coalition accept that all the business of the Scottish Executive including decisions, announcements, expenditure plans, proposed legislation and appointments should be supported collectively by all members of the Executive and that there should be an appropriate level of consultation and discussion to ensure the support of all Ministers. Ministers have the opportunity to express their views frankly as decisions are reached, and opinions expressed and advice given within the Executive remain private. However, once a decision is reached, it is to be binding on all Ministers. Any Minister who cannot accept a decision of the Executive is expected to resign. In practice, however, the doctrine has occasionally been undermined by the actions of some

---

[32] SA 1998, s 53.
[33] SA 1998, s 56.
[34] SA 1998, s 57.
[35] *Partnership for a Better Scotland* (May 2003), Section 5.

Ministers who have been unable to support decisions but who, nevertheless, remained in post[36].

EXECUTIVE DEVOLUTION IN RELATION TO RESERVED MATTERS

The White Paper made it clear that the Scottish Executive was to be responsible for the exercise of certain administrative functions in areas where the law-making powers are reserved to the UK Government. This is termed executive devolution. Prior to devolution, most of these functions were performed by the Secretary of State for Scotland. These include:

- the administration in Scotland of European Structural Funds;
- civil nuclear emergency planning;
- powers and duties in relation to electricity supply;
- administration of firearms licensing;
- establishment and operation of certain public sector pension schemes;
- enforcing medicine legislation;
- designation of casino areas;
- various powers and duties relating to transport.

In most cases these are now transferred to Scottish Ministers for them to exercise instead of UK Ministers. Some are exercisable concurrently by Scottish Ministers and UK Ministers, while others are exercised by a UK Minister, but only after consultation with, or with the consent of, the Scottish Ministers.

---

[36] Mike Watson the MSP for Glasgow Cathcart who was a Minister in 2002/03 found himself unable to accept a Cabinet decision to close a hospital in Glasgow. He did not resign, but following the election in 2003 he was not re-appointed as a Minister.

7 RELATIONS BETWEEN SCOTLAND AND WESTMINSTER

INTRODUCTION

As we have seen in Chapter 2, the Scottish Parliament has its powers devolved to it by the UK Parliament and the UK Parliament has not relinquished its sovereignty. The Scottish Parliament is, therefore, a body subordinate to the UK Parliament and could be abolished by it. However, as long as the Scottish Parliament remains popular as an institution with the Scottish people, the UK Parliament is unlikely to take such drastic action. Nevertheless, the UK Parliament retains some important controls over the Scottish Parliament.

LEGISLATIVE AND EXECUTIVE CONTROLS

As has been explained in Chapter 2, two areas reserved to the UK Parliament by Sch 5 to the Scotland Act 1998 (SA 1998) are the Union of the Kingdoms of Scotland and England and the Parliament of the UK and most of the provisions of the SA 1998 are protected from modification by Sch 4. A Scottish Executive dominated by parties in favour of independence, therefore, would not be able to pass a valid Act of the Scottish Parliament declaring Scottish independence.

The SA 1998 sets out a complex pattern of provisions designed to prevent the Scottish Parliament from passing a Bill, and Scottish Ministers from taking action, which would either be beyond the powers given by the Act, or which the UK Government would consider to be against the interests of UK defence or national security. As has already been discussed in Chapter 5, the Advocate General for Scotland, who is a Law Officer of the UK Parliament, has the power, under s 33(1) of the Act, to refer the question as to whether a Bill or any provision of a Bill is within the legislative competence of the Scottish Parliament to the Judicial Committee of the Privy Council for decision. This approach dictates that the final decision is made by judges.

In some circumstances a political, rather than a judicial, approach is considered appropriate. A Secretary of State of the UK Parliament has the power under the SA 1998, s 35 to make an order prohibiting the Presiding Officer from submitting a Bill for Royal Assent if he or she believes it would be incompatible with the UK's international obligations or its defence or national security interests. This power is also available to a Secretary of State if a Bill makes modifications to the law concerning reserved matters, as it can do in certain limited circumstances[1], and he or she is concerned such modifications may adversely affect the operation of that law[2]. A similar power is given to a Secretary of State under s 58(4).

---

[1] SA 1998, Sch 4, para 3.
[2] SA 1998, s 35.

Similarly, under s 58(1)–(3), a Secretary of State may prevent a member of the Scottish Executive from taking a proposed action or may require such a member to take action under certain circumstances. The circumstances cover situations where a UK Minister has reasonable grounds for believing that a member of the Scottish Executive is about to act in a way which is incompatible with any international obligation. On the other hand, if he or she believes that some action is required for giving effect to an international obligation, a Secretary of State can direct by order that the action be taken by a member of the Scottish Executive. Such an action might even include introducing a Bill in the Scottish Parliament although it is difficult to see how MSPs, particularly those from political parties different from that of the UK Government, could be forced to vote for such a Bill. In that case, the UK Government would probably fall back on the power of the UK Parliament, described in the following paragraphs, to make laws for Scotland and pass the Bill itself. Such a situation would lead to a serious political confrontation between the two governments and, no doubt, strenuous endeavours would be made behind the scenes to avoid such a crisis. An order made under any of the provisions of s 58 must contain reasons[3].

In addition, there are powers shared between UK Ministers of the Crown and Scottish Ministers[4] which require to be handled by liaison arrangements. Functions in relation to the observation and implementation of European Community rights and rights under the European Convention on Human Rights continue in the main to be dealt with by UK Ministers[5].

As well as this set of provisions giving the UK Government the ability to intervene in would-be legislation of the Parliament or actions of Scottish Ministers, the UK Government also has the much more direct ability to take action in Scottish matters as a result of s 28(7) of the SA 1998 which states in unequivocal terms that the power given to the Parliament does not affect the power of the UK Parliament to make laws for Scotland. Such a power allows the UK Parliament, if it were to wish to do so, not only to pass laws in relation to devolved matters, but also to change the SA 1998 itself and so change the powers of the Scottish Parliament or Scottish Ministers.

THE 'SEWEL CONVENTION' AND UK LEGISLATION ON DEVOLVED MATTERS

When the Scottish Parliament was set up, it was widely expected that these provisions allowing the UK Parliament to legislate on issues devolved to the Scottish Parliament would be used rarely[6] and that the SA 1998, s 28(7) was more likely to come into play in the event of some constitutional crisis setting the Scottish Parliament and Executive at odds.

It was always envisaged, however, that there could be instances where it would be more convenient for legislation on devolved matters to be passed by the UK

---

[3] SA 1998, s 58(5).
[4] Conferred by section 56. See ch 5.
[5] SA 1998, s 57.
[6] Donald Dewar, the first First Minister in the Scottish Parliament, said in the House of Commons when still Secretary of State for Scotland that there was 'a possibility, in theory, of the UK Parliament legislating across those [devolved] areas, but it is not one which we anticipate or expect.' (Hansard HC Debs, vol 305, cols 402–403, 28 January 1998).

Parliament[7]. The UK Government made it clear during the passage of the Scotland Bill through the UK Parliament that it was its expectation that this power would be used only with the agreement of the Scottish Parliament. This position was spelt out in the debate in the House of Lords on the Scotland Bill when the then government Minister, Lord Sewel, stated that [the government] 'would expect a convention to be established that Westminster would not normally legislate with regard to devolved matters in Scotland without the consent of the Scottish parliament'[8].

This convention, very soon to become known as the 'Sewel Convention', has in fact come into play much more regularly than one imagines its author expected. Westminster's power to legislate on devolved matters has been used extensively, but on every occasion with the consent of the Scottish Parliament expressed through a motion agreeing that the measure in question should be considered by the UK Parliament. These motions have come to be known as 'Sewel motions'. By the end of June 2002, 34 Sewel motions had been passed by the Scottish Parliament, some dealing with relatively minor pieces of legislation, but some dealing with major and substantial areas of policy[9].

There are a number of reasons why such a course of action has proved attractive to government in both Edinburgh and Westminster. First, there are many occasions in which UK Bills deal with matters which are undoubtedly reserved in general, but have a bearing on and require changes in devolved legislation to make them fully effective in Scotland. Good examples of such legislation are UK Acts of Parliament dealing with immigration and asylum matters, which are reserved, but which legislation also required changes in certain provisions devolved to the Scottish Parliament, e g in housing, education and social work[10].

Second, there are areas of policy where both the UK and the Scottish Governments have felt that a UK-wide approach to the issue concerned would be more effective than if separate approaches were to be pursued in Scotland and England. An early example of such legislation was the Food Standards Act 1999, which established a Food Standards Agency. The legislation passed through the UK Parliament after the Scottish Parliament had acquired its full powers, and food safety is a matter which is devolved to the Scottish Parliament. However, the UK and Scottish Governments decided that it would be appropriate for the legislation to be introduced on a UK-wide basis, if the Scottish Parliament consented, as it duly did. It should be noted that the Food Standards Agency does have a separate Scottish executive machinery and advisory committee, and will report to both the Scottish and UK Parliaments. Moreover, it is made clear in the Act that it

---

[7] See White Paper *Scotland's Parliament*, para 4.4.

[8] HL Debs, 21 Jul 1998, vol 592, c 791.

[9] In addition to those referred to in this chapter, Sewel motions had by the end of June 2002 been adopted to deal with the following proposed Westminster Bills: Financial Services and Markets; Electronic Communications; Limited Liability Partnerships; Sea Fishing Grants (Charges); Representation of the People; Sexual Offences (Amendment); Political Parties, Elections and Referendums; Regulation of Investigatory Powers; Learning and Skills; Race Relations (Amendment); Insolvency; Care Standards; Government Resources and Accounts; Criminal Justice and Court Services; Health and Social Care; Outworking; Criminal Justice and Police; International Development; Culture and Recreation; Armed Forces; Adoption and Children; NHS Reform and Health Care Professions; Police Reform; Enterprise; Private Hire Vehicles (Carriage of Guide Dogs etc). Some of these Bills had only minor implications for Scotland, and some of the Bills were not in fact enacted, but many of the Bills included provisions of considerable significance for Scotland.

[10] See the Immigration and Asylum Act 1999 and the Nationality, Immigration and Asylum Act 2002.

does not detract from the Scottish Parliament's right to legislate in the area of food safety if it so wishes[11]. Such a wish to ensure a UK-wide approach by government has been particularly evident in measures seeking to tackle serious crime and international crime, where on a number of occasions since 1999 the UK Parliament has passed measures which include sometimes extensive provisions affecting matters that fall within the powers of the Scottish Parliament, eg the Anti-Terrorism, Crime and Security Act 2001, and the Proceeds of Crime Act 2002. The last measure was notable for the considerable extent to which it included separate Scottish provisions, in a UK Bill, to take account of the different Scottish legal system. Other areas in which legislation on devolved matters has been passed by Westminster include those dealing with the UK's international obligations which have consequences for both reserved and devolved matters, eg the International Criminal Court Act 2001.

Another reason why the use of Sewel motions can be attractive is that if the Scottish Executive wishes to introduce legislation in Scotland to parallel legislative initiatives which are taking place elsewhere, in England, it does not need to put aside time in the Scottish Parliament's programme to allow for the passage of essentially the same legislation. That avoids a situation where such parallel legislation could not be introduced as quickly in Scotland because of lack of parliamentary time, or at the expense of other elements within the Scottish Executive's programme. Passing Scottish legislation through Westminster also has the advantage for the Executive that such legislation cannot be challenged as being ultra vires, whereas Scottish Parliament legislation can be challenged on the grounds that it goes beyond the powers of the Scottish Parliament. It is therefore an attractive route to follow in the case of legislation which the Scottish Executive fears may be challenged in the courts as being beyond its powers[12].

Regular use of these motions has been disputed, particularly, although not exclusively, by Scottish nationalists who have objected that the procedure has the effect of taking decision away making from the Scottish Parliament[13]. There has also been objection to the fact that the terms of the Sewel motion initially agreeing to Westminster legislating are very broad, and although the motion is normally accompanied by a memorandum setting out the purpose and effect of the proposed Westminster Bill in more detail, which memorandum can be the subject of debate in the Scottish Parliament in committee, it does not appear that there is always extensive debate in committee on the terms of such memoranda. Moreover, the eventual legislation which emerges from Westminster may eventually be amended to a substantial degree so that it varies considerably from the legislation that the Scottish Parliament originally thought it was consenting to being dealt with at UK level. Although it has been accepted by government at both Westminster and Scottish level that, if there are substantial changes made at Westminster subsequent to the agreement to a Sewel motion by the Scottish Parliament, the Scottish Parliament might have the opportunity to look at the issue

---

[11] Food Standards Act 1999, s 35(3).

[12] See memorandum by Scotland Office to Scottish Parliament Procedures Committee inquiry into the Sewel convention, Office of the Deputy Prime Minister, October 2002. See also Written Memorandum given in evidence by Professor Alan Page to the House of Lords Select Committee on the Constitution's Inquiry into *Devolution: Inter-Institutional Relations in the United Kingdom*, HL Paper 147, July 2002, p 185, para 12.

[13] See eg, the comments by SNP MSP Mike Russell in Scottish Parliament Official Report, 30 January 2002, c5881–5882.

again, this has in practice happened rarely[14]. On the other hand, the fact that the Sewel convention has now been well established means that any attempt by Westminster to use its powers to legislate on devolved Scottish matters *without* the consent of the Scottish Parliament expressed through a 'Sewel motion' would stand out much more clearly as a measure which was being imposed on Scotland without Scottish consent, which would presumably make such a course of action even more politically difficult for any UK Government that considered taking such a drastic step.

Whether the use of Sewel motions will continue at its present level is an open question. If the current or an increasing level of use of the procedure continues, there may well be calls (even by those other than nationalists) at least to make clear the extent to which the original Sewel motion needs to be re-approved by the Scottish Parliament in the event of substantial amendment through the subsequent passage of the relevant legislation at Westminster.

It is clear, however, that although 'Sewel motions' and the 'Sewel Convention' are to be found nowhere in the White Paper or the SA 1998, and 'Sewel motions' have no special status within the Scottish Parliament's procedures, both have become an important part of the constitutional arrangements underpinning Scottish devolution. The regular use of Sewel motions may simply reflect the fact that much political debate and media coverage, along with much of the activity of government and the political establishment, still takes place at a UK, or at least a British, level, notwithstanding the growth of devolved political institutions in many parts of the UK. The Scottish electorate may at times be attracted by policies being promoted in England, and influence the Scottish Executive to introduce policy initiatives broadly similar to those being promoted elsewhere in the UK. There is, it has been suggested, an inevitable pressure for uniformity which will tend to limit deviation from the UK norm in the case of legislation and government activity alike[15].

Of course, one of the factors making regular use of the Sewel procedure possible is the fact that the administrations in both Westminster and Edinburgh have, since the inception of devolution, been Labour-led. If the Scottish Parliament and Executive were to be of a different political composition to that of the government in Westminster, one can imagine that the use of Sewel motions might become much more limited than at present – although it is to be noted that even the SNP do not appear to be opposed to the use of Sewel motions in all circumstances.

In contrast to the regular use of the Sewel motion procedure, and no doubt as a result of the similar political leadership in both Scotland and at UK level, the UK Government has not found it necessary to make any use of the various provisions described above[16] allowing it to stop the passage of proposed legislation through the Scottish Parliament, or to intervene in the activity of Scottish Ministers.

---

[14] On these workings of the Sewel convention, see Professor Alan Page, (see n 12) pp 183–186, and also his Oral Evidence (see n 12), pp 186–195; Alan Page and Andrea Batey, *Scotland's other Parliament: Westminster legislation about devolved matters in Scotland since devolution,* Public Law, Autumn 2002, pp 501–523; Cabinet Office Devolution Guidance Note 10, http:www.devolution. odpm.gov.uk/dgn/pdf/dg10/pdf; and Oral Evidence given by George Foulkes MP, Minister of State at the Scotland Office, to House of Commons Scottish Affairs Committee, 7 November 2001, qs 17–18.

[15] See article by Alan Page and Andrea Batey, (see n 14) pp 521–523.

[16] See pp 84–85.

LIAISON ARRANGEMENTS

If the various executive and legislative controls described above were ever to become used on a frequent basis, that would be an indication that the devolution settlement was under strain. The clear hope of the Government when it launched its proposals for a Scottish Parliament was that a good working relationship between the UK Government and the Scottish Executive would allow areas of difficulty to be dealt with at an early stage, through joint working, consultation, and other more informal mechanisms, and thereby avoid the need for what would almost inevitably be a controversial use by central government of its ultimate executive and legislative supremacy. In order to put such arrangements on a firm footing, the UK Government has entered into a number of agreements with the Scottish Ministers (and the other devolved administrations in the UK) which seek to set out the terms on which the different administrations will work together, at both political and official levels[17].

Although the texts establishing these arrangements described them as 'agreements', it should be noted that it is clearly stated that the agreements should not be legally binding. It is also clear that the agreements are not intended to give either the various administrations which are signatories to them, nor indeed any other individual or corporate person, any rights which they can enforce through legal proceedings. They are instead statements of principle, intended to be 'binding in honour only'. Notwithstanding their non-binding nature, however, the various agreements are of great practical significance in setting down the basis on which the devolved administrations will work with the UK Government. Moreover, the very terminology of the agreements is clearly designed to give them a special status, marking them out as having a constitutional significance beyond the ordinary government document. Indeed, although the agreements make it clear that they do not create new legal rights and obligations, one might expect that in due course attempts could be made in court proceedings to suggest that they can at least be used to provide a background against which a particular action of a Minister can be judged, although so far there does not seem to have been any attempt to do so.

The main elements of these arrangements are now described.

The principal agreement is the Memorandum of Understanding which sets out the principles that are to underlie relations between the UK Government and the devolved administrations, and contains a number of important provisions.

- It commits the various administrations to seek to alert each other to relevant developments within their areas of responsibility; to give appropriate consideration to the views of each other's administration; and, where appropriate, where there is shared responsibility, to establish arrangements that allow for policies to be drawn up jointly between the administrations.
- It makes provisions for the exchange of information, statistics and research.
- It places on each of the administrations a responsibility to respect any confidentiality restrictions imposed by the provider of any information.

---

[17] See *Devolution: memorandum of understanding and supplementary agreements between the United Kingdom Government, Scottish Ministers and the Cabinet of the National Assembly of Wales,* Cm 5240. The memorandum contains the underlying agreement together with the first 'concordats'.

- It affirms as a convention that the UK Parliament would not normally legislate on devolved matters without the agreement of the devolved legislature. However, the UK Parliament retains the right to discuss any devolved matter, and similarly the Scottish Parliament, and the other devolved assemblies, will be entitled to debate non-devolved matters.
- It affirms that the legal controls over the Scottish Parliament and the other devolved assemblies are to be used by the UK Government as a last resort only.

The Memorandum also established a Joint Ministerial Committee. This comprises the UK Prime Minister, the Scottish and Northern Ireland First Ministers, the Welsh First Secretary (together in all cases with a deputy or other colleague) and the Secretaries of State for Northern Ireland, Scotland, and Wales, together with other members of the various administrations as appropriate. It was originally envisaged that the Joint Ministerial Committee would meet in this structure on a plenary basis at least once a year, but in practice it has met a little less frequently[18]. In addition, the Joint Ministerial Committee may meet in other 'functional' formats: for example, if dealing with environment issues, it will be comprised of the relevant Environment Ministers, and if agriculture, the relevant Agriculture Ministers.

The Joint Ministerial Committee is to meet for two purposes: first, to take stock of the way that devolution is working, either generally or in a particular area; and, second, to deal with particular problems between two or more administrations (if other attempts to resolve them have been unsuccessful). The committee is staffed by a Joint Secretariat, and is shadowed by a committee of officials from the various administrations. The Secretariat and Committee prepare matters for meetings, and also allow for contact and discussion at official level on the manner in which the devolution arrangements are working, again both in general terms and in the context of any particular difficulty that might arise. In practice, potential differences between the various administrations have been resolved at official level in the Secretariat, or the committee of officials, rather than in the Joint Ministerial Committee itself.

Accompanying the Memorandum and the Joint Ministerial Committee are the Concordats, which seek to set out detailed working arrangements between the different administrations. Four Concordats were drawn up shortly after the first elections to the Scottish Parliament and the National Assembly for Wales, to deal with matters affecting all the devolved administrations, with the aim of providing a broadly similar framework applicable for them all. These cover the following areas of government activity:

- Co-ordination of European Union Policy Issues
- Financial Assistance to Industry
- International Relations
- Statistics.

In addition to these broad-ranging concordats, it was also agreed that bilateral concordats be set up between individual UK Government departments and their

---

[18] See evidence by John Prescott MP, Deputy Prime Minister, to the House of Lords Select Committee on the Constitution's Inquiry into *Devolution: Inter-Institutional Relations in the United Kingdom*, HL Paper 147, July 2002, p 27, q 55.

Scottish and Welsh counterparts to deal with working relationships on a more detailed basis, and a large number of such agreements have been drawn up[19]. Such agreements can be entered into by two or more administrations as and when they are required, and no doubt as time goes by new issues will arise which will result in new concordats being put in place.

These various arrangements are backed up by a number of Devolution Guidance Notes produced by the UK Cabinet Office[20]. These deal with matters such as the way in which bilateral relations between different administrations should be conducted, correspondence, ministerial accountability, how to conduct parliamentary business when it concerns an item which is the responsibility of a different Parliament or Assembly, and the notification of legislative proposals. It is pointed out in Devolution Guidance Note 1 that, although concordats are intended to regulate many working relationships between different administrations, other, less formal, arrangements (or simply ad hoc arrangements) will be appropriate in many cases, and in practice such less formal arrangements appear to have been of much more significance in ensuring good working relations between Westminster and the devolved administrations rather than the more formal liaison machinery set out in the Memorandum of Understanding[21].

In addition to these arrangements, it should also be noted that the Secretary of State for Scotland (as with the other territorial Secretaries of State) was originally envisaged as continuing to play an important role as a channel of communication between the UK Government and the Scottish Executive at the highest level. Indeed, the Memorandum of Understanding gives these Secretaries of State a specific role in trying to resolve differences between the UK Government and a devolved administration before it requires to be considered by the Joint Ministerial Committee. It remains to be seen how the new Ministerial and departmental arrangements following the diminution in the position of the Secretary of State for Scotland in June 2003 will affect both the terms of the Memorandum of Understanding and the workings of the liaison arrangements[22].

FINANCIAL CONTROLS

The financing of the Scottish Parliament is dealt with in detail in Chapter 8. Suffice it to say at this point that the UK Government and Parliament retain tight financial controls over the Scottish Parliament. Most of the Scottish Parliament's expenditure is financed by a block grant determined annually by the Treasury. The Treasury also has the power to require the Scottish Ministers to provide any information it may reasonably request.

The Scottish Parliament has only very limited tax-raising powers; powers which are as strictly, if not more, constrained than the tax-raising powers of local government. The SA describes these as 'tax-varying' powers. The Parliament has

---

[19] By early 2002 more than 40 such concordats had been drawn up between Westminster and the various devolved administrations, of which 18 affected Scotland.

[20] See Written Evidence by the Cabinet Office to the House of Lords Select Committee on the Constitution's Inquiry into *Devolution: Inter-Institutional Relations in the United Kingdom*, HL Paper 147, July 2002, p 17 para 33 and Annex B.

[21] See e g the Oral Evidence given by Patricia Ferguson MSP, Minister for Parliamentary Business, to the House of Lords Select Committee on the Constitution's Inquiry into *Devolution: Inter-Institutional Relations in the United Kingdom*, HL Paper 147, July 2002, pp 113–114.

[22] See pp 92–93.

the power, under s 73, to vary the rate of income tax paid by Scottish taxpayers upwards or downwards by 3p in the pound. At current rates this means an increase or decrease in the monies available of only about £870m. As discussed in Chapter 8, the governing coalition during the first term of the Scottish Parliament, which was re-elected in 2003, has made it clear that it has no intention of using these tax-varying powers in any event.

The SA 1998 requires the Scottish Parliament to make provision by legislation for financial control, accounts and audit[23] and one of the first measures introduced into the Parliament was a Bill to deal with such matters[24].

THE OFFICE OF THE SECRETARY OF STATE FOR SCOTLAND

The office of the Secretary of State for Scotland has a long history, dating back to the days before the union of the Scottish and English Parliaments in 1707. After the Jacobite rebellion of 1745, the office lapsed in the following year and the Lord Advocate became the chief Scottish Minister. This arrangement lasted until 1885 when the office of Secretary for Scotland and a Scottish Office were re-established. In 1892 the Secretary for Scotland was given a seat in the Cabinet and has retained that seat ever since except in time of war. In 1926, the title was changed to that of Secretary of State for Scotland. In 1939, St Andrew's House in Edinburgh was opened as the headquarters of the Scottish Office and the powers of the Scottish Office were directly vested in the Secretary of State.

There are many references to the Secretary of State in the SA 1998. As has been explained above[25], the offices of Secretary of State are interchangeable and in some cases the powers conferred by the SA 1998 will be exercisable by other Ministers of the Crown. The Secretary of State for Scotland was given many important powers to be exercised in the seven months between the passing of the SA 1998 and the formal opening of the Scottish Parliament by the Queen on 1 July 1999. However, when the Parliament received its full legislative powers and most of the powers of the Secretary of State were transferred to the Scottish Executive, the role of the Secretary of State was undoubtedly diminished. The size of the ministerial team was cut to reflect the reduced legislative and executive powers over Scottish matters remaining with the UK Government and Parliament. During the Scottish Parliament's first term from 1999 to 2003, the two Scottish Secretaries (first John Reid, and then Helen Liddell) emphasised the continuing importance of the post in Scotland's public life, and the post continued to be of some importance in Scotland's political life. However, the continued existence of the post was criticised as anomalous by many commentators and opposition politicians (and privately by some within the governing Labour Party also).

It was therefore no great surprise when the Prime Minister, Tony Blair, took the opportunity during a government reshuffle in June 2003 to alter significantly the role of the Secretary of State for Scotland. Although the post remained, it was added to the existing responsibilities of another member of the Cabinet who also represented a Scottish constituency (Alistair Darling, the Secretary of State for Transport). (The post of Secretary of State for Wales was similarly combined with

---

[23] SA 1998, s 70.

[24] *Public Finance and Accountability (Scotland) Act 2000*, introduced in the Parliament on 7 September 1999, and enacted 17 January 2000.

[25] See p 82.

another Cabinet post, although the post of Secretary of State for Northern Ireland was retained, due to the continuing suspension of devolved government within Northern Ireland). However, the Scotland Office (successor to the Scottish Office) was abolished as a separate department, and taken under the umbrella of a new Department for Constitutional Affairs now headed by its own Secretary of State. A full-time junior Minister for Scottish Affairs was retained, although this post is similarly to be located in the new department. It is not yet clear how the new arrangements for representing Scottish interests at Westminster will work out in practice, and they have a number of anomalous features (eg, the fact that the Scotland Office will report to the Secretary of State for Scotland, even though the office and its staff are now situated in the Department for Constitutional Affairs). It may well be that in due course the very title of Secretary of State for Scotland might be abolished, perhaps with the junior Minister for Scottish Affairs being given some upgraded status and responsibilities as a consequence.

It is too early to say what other consequences might flow from the change in the status, and perhaps eventual abolition, of the post of Secretary of State for Scotland. The disappearance of its intermediary role may lead to the Scottish Executive needing to increase its own direct lobbying for and promotion of Scotland's interests in government circles at UK level, which might lead to an increased use of the various liaison arrangements described earlier in this chapter.

CONCLUSION

The first years of the Scottish Parliament have shown, therefore, that it is possible for devolution to operate without any major conflict between governments and legislatures at Westminster and in Scotland, and indeed with hardly any need to make use of the mechanisms set up after 1999 to ensure liaison and co-operation between the two tiers. However, the use of 'Sewel motions' and the changes to the role of the Scottish Secretary (the former unexpected at the time that the devolved arrangements were being set up; the latter less unexpected) emphasise how in this area, as in many others, Scotland's new constitutional relationship with the rest of the United Kingdom continues to evolve, even without changing any of the parameters of the underlying devolution legislation itself.

8 LEGAL CHALLENGES TO ACTS OF THE SCOTTISH PARLIAMENT AND ACTIONS OF THE SCOTTISH EXECUTIVE

INTRODUCTION

As we have seen in previous chapters[1], the Scotland Act 1998 (SA 1998) contains detailed provisions designed to ensure that the Scottish Parliament does not seek to pass legislation outwith its competence. These are reinforced by numerous mechanisms allowing the UK Government to intervene if the Scottish Parliament or Executive do stray beyond the boundaries of the powers conferred on them by statute. There is always the possibility, however, that a provision which is beyond the Parliament's powers may slip through the net, and as a result there will be a wish to challenge that provision even though it has passed through all its stages in the Parliament (including the receipt of Royal Assent). Similarly, there will be occasions when a particular action taken on behalf of the Scottish Executive might be claimed to be invalid as being outside the authority given to it by the SA 1998. Such legal challenges to the validity of provisions could potentially arise in a wide range of circumstances. They could involve disputes between the Scottish Executive and the UK Government, between an individual and the Scottish Executive or between two individuals. To date, however, all the challenges to the validity of Acts of the Scottish Parliament or actions of the Scottish Executive have arisen from individuals or from private organisations.

DEVOLUTION ISSUES

Such questions as to whether Acts of the Scottish Parliament or actions of the Scottish Executive have strayed beyond their powers are described in the SA 1998 as 'devolution issues' and Sch 6 to the Act sets out in considerable detail both what constitutes a 'devolution issue' and how such issues are to be handled. A 'devolution issue' can arise before virtually any court or tribunal, in civil or in criminal cases.

Part I of Schedule 6 first defines a devolution issue as 'a question whether an Act of the Scottish Parliament or any provision of an Act of the Scottish Parliament is within the legislative competence of the Parliament'. However, as mentioned above, a devolution issue may arise in areas other than Acts of the Scottish Parliament. For example, questions of legislative competence may arise over the executive actions of Scottish Ministers. Schedule 6 further defines devolution issues as including the following:

- a question whether any function is a function of the Scottish Ministers, the First Minister or the Lord Advocate;

---

[1] Chapters 5 and 7.

- a question whether the purported or proposed exercise of a function by a member of the Scottish Executive is, or would be, within devolved competence;
- a question whether a purported or proposed exercise of a function by a member of the Scottish Executive is, or would be, incompatible with any rights under the European Convention on Human Rights or with European Community (EC) law;
- a question whether a failure to act by a member of the Scottish Executive is incompatible with any of the rights under the European Convention on Human Rights or with EC law;
- any other question about whether a function is exercisable within devolved competence in or as regards Scotland and any other question arising by virtue of the SA 1998 about reserved matters.

However, a devolution issue is not to be taken to arise in any legal proceedings simply because one of the parties argues that it does if the court considers that contention to be 'frivolous or vexatious'[2].

Since the SA 1998 came into force and the setting up of the Scottish Parliament and Executive, there have been a large number of cases in which 'devolution issues' have been raised. The vast majority have been raised as challenges to actions of the Lord Advocate in his capacity as head of the criminal prosecution system in Scotland, alleging that he or someone acting on his behalf (eg a procurator fiscal) has brought or is conducting a prosecution that is in some way incompatible with the European Convention on Human Rights and that such prosecution is as a result invalid (because the Lord Advocate, as a member of the Scottish Executive, has no power to act in a way which is incompatible with Convention rights[3]). Almost all the other challenges to actions of the Scottish Executive have also been made on grounds that such actions breach 'Convention rights' in some way. There have been few challenges to an Act of the Scottish Parliament itself, as distinct from some action taken under the authority of a member of the Scottish Executive. One such challenge was made (unsuccessfully) very soon after the Parliament came into being, when an effort was made to strike down the Mental Health (Public Safety and Appeals) (Scotland) Act 1999[4]. Another significant challenge to Scottish Parliament legislation was the attack by foxhunters on the Parliament's competence to pass the Protection of Wild Mammals (Scotland) Act 2002[5]. Interestingly, both these challenges were also based on claims that the legislation in question breached certain of the Convention rights.

HUMAN RIGHTS LEGISLATION AND THE SCOTLAND ACT 1998

The fact that virtually all the challenges described above have been based on a claim that the Scottish Parliament or Executive has breached a 'Convention right'

---

[2] SA 1998, Sch 6, para 2.

[3] SA 1998, s 57(2).

[4] *Anderson, Doherty and Reid v Scottish Ministers and Advocate General for Scotland* 2000 SLT 873.

[5] The challenge was unsuccessful in the Outer House of the Court of Session (see *Adams v The Scottish Ministers* 2003 SLT 366), but has been appealed.

illustrates the close interrelationship between the SA 1998 and the Human Rights Act 1998 (HRA 1998). Indeed, for the first year and a half of the new devolved arrangements, Scotland was in the somewhat strange position of being the only part of the United Kingdom in which the European Convention on Human Rights had been partially incorporated into domestic law. This was because the provisions of the SA 1998 requiring legislation, and actions of the Scottish Executive (including, of course, actions of those acting on behalf of its members), to be compatible with the European Convention on Human Rights came into effect when the Scottish Parliament and the members of the Scottish Executive acquired their respective powers in stages in mid-1999. By contrast, the date when the HRA 1998, which incorporated 'Convention rights' into UK law, was to come into force was delayed until October 2000. To allow for the fact that the HRA 1998 was expected to come into force after the provisions of the SA 1998 did so, the latter laid down that the Convention rights as provided for in the HRA 1998 would apply to the relevant sections of the SA 1998 as if the HRA were in force[6]. The practical effect of these provisions is that the Convention rights became incorporated into Scots law as far as devolved matters were concerned as soon as executive and legislative powers were transferred to the Scottish Parliament and Executive in the summer of 1999. It was therefore hardly surprising that the opportunity to raise alleged breaches of Convention rights as devolution issues was taken up so extensively given the fact that it was not initially possible to make use of the HRA 1998.

After the HRA 1998 came into force, there was some uncertainty as to whether a claim that an action of the Scottish Executive was incompatible with the European Convention on Human Rights could be raised under the HRA 1998 as well as, or instead of, being raised as a 'devolution issue'. However, the Judicial Committee of the Privy Council has now made it clear that such a challenge *must* be raised as a 'devolution issue' and cannot be raised under the HRA 1998[7]. The case does not deal with the question of whether a challenge to the competence of an Act of the Scottish Parliament on the grounds of incompatibility with Convention rights also has to be taken as a devolution issue only, but the logic of the decision strongly suggests that would be the case.

LEGAL PROCEEDINGS IN SCOTLAND

Part II of Sch 6 to the SA 1998 deals with legal proceedings in Scotland (those in England and Wales are dealt with in Part III, and in Northern Ireland in Part IV). Proceedings may be instituted by the Advocate General (ie the UK Government's Law Officer for Scotland) or the Lord Advocate. The Lord Advocate may defend proceedings instituted by the Advocate General. A court or tribunal must order intimation of any devolution issue arising before it to the Lord Advocate and the Advocate General and they may take part as a party in the proceedings so far as they relate to a devolution issue.

In civil proceedings before a lower court (ie the sheriff court or the Outer House of the Court of Session) or a tribunal, a devolution issue which arises may be referred to the Inner House of the Court of Session. A tribunal from which there is no right of appeal must make such a reference. In criminal proceedings before

---

[6] SA 1998, s 129(2).
[7] *HMA v R* 2003 SLT 4.

the district courts, the sheriff court or before a single judge in the High Court, a devolution issue, if it arises, may be referred to a larger bench of judges in the High Court of Justiciary. A comprehensive set of rules has been brought into effect specifying how devolution issues are to be raised in both the lower courts and the Scottish appeal courts, and how appeals from the lower courts should be dealt with[8].

Any court consisting of three or more judges of the Court of Session (normally a civil appeal court) or two or more judges of the High Court of Justiciary (a court of criminal appeal) may refer a devolution issue to the Judicial Committee of the Privy Council, unless the issue has been referred to either of them by a lower court, in which case the issue must be decided by the superior court. Where the Court of Session has decided a devolution issue referred to it by a lower court, an appeal lies to the Judicial Committee.

There are two courts in Scotland from which there is normally no further appeal to the House of Lords. These are the High Court of Justiciary, sitting as a court of criminal appeal, and the Lands Valuation Appeal Court. If a decision on a devolution issue has been made by one of these courts, an appeal may be made to the Judicial Committee with the leave of the court concerned or with special leave of the Judicial Committee[9]. Cases involving devolution issues started to come before the Judicial Committee from early 2000, and by mid-2002 nine cases had reached it.

It is likely, however, that the role of the Privy Council in dealing with devolution issues will be short-lived. That is because in the summer of 2003 the UK Government announced that it would be proposing the establishment of a new Supreme Court for the UK. This new court would take over both the function of the Appellate Committee of the House of Lords, including its role as the final court of appeal for Scottish civil cases, and the functions of the Judicial Committee of the Privy Council in respect of devolution issues[10].

At the time of writing, Sch 6 to the SA 1998 provides that if a devolution issue arises in judicial proceedings in the House of Lords it is to be referred to the Judicial Committee unless the House of Lords consider it more appropriate to determine the issue themselves. (Presumably this provision will become superfluous and will accordingly be removed if the functions of the Judicial Committee on devolution issues are transferred to the new Supreme Court.)

The Law Officers of Scotland, England and Northern Ireland may require a court or tribunal before which a devolution issue has arisen to refer it to the Judicial Committee. A direct reference to the Judicial Committee may also be made by the Law Officers of Scotland, England and Northern Ireland of a devolution issue which is not the subject of legal proceedings. This will involve the judges in ruling on hypothetical issues, rather than on concrete facts – an extremely unusual procedure for British judges.

---

[8] Act of Adjournal (Devolution Issues Rules) 1999, SI 1999/1346 (for criminal matters); Act of Sederunt (Devolution Issues Rules) 1999, SI 1999/1345 (for civil matters, Court of Session); Act of Sederunt (Proceedings for Determination of Devolution Issues Rules) 1999, SI 1999/1347 (for civil matters, sheriff court).

[9] The rules of procedure for such appeals and references are set out in the Judicial Committee (Devolution Issues) Rules Order 1999, SI 1999/665).

[10] *Constitutional Reform: A Supreme Court for the United Kingdom*, A Department for Constitutional Affairs Consultation Paper, July 2003, www.lcd.gov.uk/consult/supremecourt/index.htm.

Any decision of the Judicial Committee in proceedings under the SA 1998 is to be stated in open court and is to be binding in all legal proceedings except those before the Judicial Committee itself[11]. This would appear to be a fairly unusual example of statute laying down rules of judicial precedent which must be followed by judges sitting in courts below the Judicial Committee.

The SA 1998 also includes a provision for subordinate legislation to be made by a UK Minister to remedy ultra vires provisions in Acts of the Scottish Parliament[12]. Subordinate legislation may also be made to remedy any improper exercise of functions by Scottish Ministers. Such subordinate legislation may be retrospective in effect[13]. This can remedy any problems which have arisen and put third parties into the position they thought they were in before the flaw in the Act or subordinate legislation was discovered. There is a further provision in the SA 1998, s 102 which allows any court or tribunal to remove, limit or suspend any retrospective effect of their decision that a provision of an Act of the Scottish Parliament or subordinate legislation is ultra vires. One of the criteria the court or tribunal must take into account in making an order under this section is the extent to which persons not party to the proceedings would otherwise be adversely affected. The Lord Advocate and any other appropriate Law Officer must be given notice of an intention to make such an order and the opportunity to be party to the proceedings as they relate to the order.

The Scottish Parliament is not the first experiment in devolution in the UK. After the partition of Ireland, a Northern Ireland Parliament was established in 1921 and continued in existence until 1972. By and large the Members of that Parliament were content with the powers which had been conferred. They tried to avoid constitutional tension by seeking the co-operation of the UK Parliament and generally found co-operation there. The courts were rarely called upon to resolve disputes. Although a number of challenges were made, only one had much success[14]. To date, there have been no successful challenges to the competency of Acts of the Scottish Parliament, and no such challenge has been made at the instance of either Members of the Scottish Parliament or the Scottish Executive. In that respect, therefore, the Scottish experience has been similar to that of Northern Ireland. However, the frequency of challenges, almost invariably on 'human rights' grounds, to the competence of actions of the Scottish Executive, and in particular the Lord Advocate, has kept the Scottish courts very busy considering the terms of the SA 1998. Although successful challenges have been few and far between, those that have been successful have sometimes had significant consequences, as has already been described[15].

---

[11] SA 1998, s 103.
[12] SA 1998, s 107.
[13] SA 1998, s 114(3).
[14] *Ulster Transport Authority v James Brown & Son Ltd* [1953] NI 79.
[15] As in *Starrs v Ruxton; Ruxton v Starrs* 2000 JC 208. See p 77; p 135, n 21.

9 FINANCING THE SCOTTISH PARLIAMENT

INTRODUCTION

The two principal sources of finance for the Scottish Parliament and the Scottish Administration are the 'block grant' allocated to it by the UK Government and Parliament, and a supplement to UK income tax to be paid by Scottish taxpayers, if the Scottish Parliament chooses to levy such a supplement. If it so wishes, the Parliament *can* also reduce the level of income tax to be paid by such taxpayers, with a corresponding reduction in the level of finance available to it.

THE BLOCK GRANT

In *Scotland's Parliament*, the government made it clear that it envisaged that the main source of finance for the Parliament would be the block grant. The block grant is a grant paid by the UK Treasury to the Scottish Office. The level of the block grant is decided from year to year in accordance with a formula which decides the balance of government spending between Scotland, England and Wales. This is known as the 'Barnett formula', named after the Chief Secretary to the Treasury in 1978 when the formula was devised to take account of the plans for devolution at that time. The Barnett formula took account of the fact that at the time it was devised, government spending was relatively higher in Scotland (and Wales) than in England[1]. The formula aimed, at least in theory, to bring about a gradual convergence between the relative levels of government spending in Scotland, Wales and England. In fact, for many years, primarily due to the fact that Scotland's share of the total Great Britain population is declining, it appeared as if that convergence might never actually take place. However, the substantial increases in public expenditure introduced by the Labour government after 1997, particularly in the 2002 Spending Round, has meant that, in theory at least, convergence could be achieved within a decade or two.

Although there have been suggestions from time to time that there should be some independent method of deciding the appropriate level of government grant to Scotland in relation to that of other parts of the UK, no such provision has yet been adopted[2]. The Scotland Act 1998 (SA 1998) has nothing to say about the level of the block grant, or how the level of government expenditure in Scotland should relate to that of the rest of the UK. The current block grant, decided in the light of the Barnett formula, will therefore continue to be the main constituent of the finance available to the new Parliament and the Scottish Government.

---

[1] After the 1992 General Election, the formula was revised to a limited extent by Michael Portillo (then Chief Secretary to the Treasury). Also see *Scotland's Parliament: Fundamentals for a New Scotland Act* (Constitution Unit, 1996) for a useful discussion of the financial arrangements for devolution.

[2] *Scotland's Parliament*, ch 5.

As the level of grant and the formula are left to the UK Government and Parliament, the SA 1998 requires to make only limited provision to allow the current system to be applied to the new Parliament. It simply establishes a Scottish Consolidated Fund, and gives to the Secretary of State the powers to make payments into that Fund 'out of money provided by [the UK] Parliament of such amounts as he may determine'[3]. The Secretary of State will presumably make such payments in line with the Barnett formula until and unless the UK Government decides on a different basis for the allocation of funds to Scotland.

The SA 1998 specifically restricts the powers of the Scottish Executive to borrow money, which means that neither it nor the Parliament can circumvent the limited powers to vary taxes by attempting to borrow money for its programmes. The Scottish Ministers have a limited power to borrow money from the Secretary of State to cover a *temporary* shortfall in the Scottish Consolidated Fund, or to provide a working balance in that fund. Otherwise, they can only borrow money under the authority of an Act of the UK Parliament[4].

As one would expect, the SA 1998 also contains a number of arrangements primarily of a technical nature to ensure that the Scottish Parliament and Executive use the finances available to them in a proper manner. Money may only be paid out of the Scottish Consolidated Fund for expenditure for which the Act or other legislation gives authority[5]. The SA 1998 obliged the Scottish Parliament to introduce legislation requiring the Scottish Ministers to prepare accounts of their income and expenditure, and to lay accounts and report on them before the Parliament. Legislation to that effect – the Public Finance and Accountability (Scotland) Act 2000, which received the Royal Assent on 17 January 2000 – was passed early in the life of the Parliament. Its provisions include the establishment of Audit Scotland, which provides a single public sector audit service, comprising existing staff of the Accounts Commission for Scotland and the Scottish staff of the National Audit Office. The SA 1998 also provided for the appointment by the Crown, on the nomination of the Scottish Parliament, of an Auditor General for Scotland, with duties which include the responsibility to examine and report on the accounts of income and expenditure of the Scottish Executive. The first Auditor General for Scotland was nominated in September 1999[6]. The Auditor General for Scotland also has a duty to examine the 'economy, efficiency, and effectiveness' with which the Scottish Ministers, the Lord Advocate, or any other person or organisation who has received money from the Scottish Consolidated Fund, have used the funds available to them[7]. Accordingly, the Public Finance and Accountability (Scotland) Act 2000 gives the Auditor General for Scotland the power to commission financial audit and value for money studies across much of the public sector in Scotland. The audit of local authorities, however, will continue to be supervised by the Accounts Commission for Scotland, and their audit reports will not be submitted to the Parliament. (As the Accounts Commission's staff are transferred by the Scottish legislation to Audit Scotland, it uses that body's services to carry out this supervisory function.)

The SA 1998 also contains a transitional provision which applies in cases where the Secretary of State has lent funds from the UK National Loans Fund

---

[3] SA 1998, s 64.
[4] SA 1998, s 66.
[5] SA 1998, s 65.
[6] The person appointed, Robert Black, was at that time the current Controller of Audit.
[7] SA 1998, s 70.

prior to the establishment of the Parliament. If the power under which the Secretary of State had made such loans has been transferred to the Scottish Ministers, any repayment of capital or interest on the loan will now be paid to the Scottish Ministers and the Scottish Consolidated Fund, with a matching adjustment to be made in the sums payable by the Secretary of State to the Scottish Ministers[8].

THE POWER TO VARY INCOME TAX

By contrast with the limited number of provisions allowing a block grant to be paid to the new Scottish Government, the arrangements set out in the SA 1998 to allow the Parliament to raise its own taxes are comprehensive. That had to be so, as the power to levy taxes is one of the powers which are otherwise reserved to the UK Parliament[9].

The power to raise taxes is contained in Part IV of the Act. The power allows the Parliament to increase or decrease the basic rate of UK tax for 'Scottish taxpayers'. The maximum that the Parliament can so vary the basic tax rate is 3p in the pound, but the Parliament can vary the tax rate by a lesser amount if it wishes. The variation can only be for whole or half pennies. If the Parliament wishes to use the power, it has to pass a resolution to that effect for each year it wishes to do so. It should be noted that the maximum variation is not linked to the actual level at which the basic tax rate is set for the UK in any one year. This means that the proportionate effect of a Scottish variation on the total basic tax rate may vary significantly from year to year. For example, if the basic tax rate is 20p in the pound, a 3p variation would mean a variation in the tax rate of 15 per cent. If the basic rate were 30p in the pound, the variation in the tax rate would be only 10 per cent.

It will be seen that the tax-varying power applies only to 'Scottish taxpayers'. Accordingly, the SA 1998 requires to define such a person, and does so in a complex set of provisions set out in s 75. The Act should be referred to for its precise provisions, but the basic definition is as follows[10]: a Scottish taxpayer is an individual who in the relevant year is resident for income tax purposes in the UK *and* Scotland is the part of the UK with which he has the 'closest connection' in that year.

An individual's 'closest connection' is with Scotland if: (1) the number of days which he or she spends in Scotland in that year is equal to or exceeds the number of days spent elsewhere in the United Kingdom; *and/or* (2) he or she (a) spends at least part of the relevant year in Scotland; *and* (b) for at least part of the time spent in Scotland, his or her principal UK home is in Scotland and he or she makes use of it as a place of residence; *and* (c) the total time in that year that such a person's principal UK home is in Scotland is as least as much as the times when his or her principal UK home is not in Scotland. The SA 1998 seeks to give definitions of what is meant by 'spending a day' and 'principal UK home'.

The purpose of the definition is to ensure that all those who might reasonably be regarded as Scottish taxpayers are liable to the tax, without catching also more

---

[8] SA 1998, s 71.

[9] SA 1998, Sch 5, Pt II, s A1.

[10] For some comments on how the tax-varying power might operate, see Sandra Eden, 'Taxing Times Ahead for the Scots' 1998 SLT (News) 57.

transient persons such as the occasional holiday visitor. It seeks to deal with some of the possible anomalies which might arise if the Scottish Parliament does indeed exercise its powers to vary the basic tax rate from that levied in England. So, for example, a person who lives in Dumfries, but travels every day to work in Carlisle, will normally be a Scottish taxpayer (although that person's colleagues may well be paying a different tax rate if they live in Carlisle); and a person who lives in Edinburgh, but commutes each week to work (and stays overnight) in London from Monday to Friday, will usually still be regarded as a Scottish taxpayer. However, a person who normally resides outside Scotland, but who has a holiday home in Scotland, will in most situations not qualify as a Scottish taxpayer. (In addition, a member of the Scottish Parliament, or a UK or European MP representing a Scottish constituency will automatically be regarded as having his or her 'closest connection' with Scotland.)

There are a number of other important features to note about the arrangements made in the Act for the use of the power to vary income tax:

- 'Scottish taxpayer' is defined as being an *individual*[11];
- income from savings and distributions, as defined in s 73 of the SA 1998, is excluded from income to which the tax-varying power applies (so that any such income will not be liable to any increase in tax if a Scottish Parliament uses its power to raise taxes)[12];
- a proposal that the tax-varying power should be used can only be put to the Parliament by a member of the Scottish Executive (and so the power could not be used at the instigation of an opposition party, or an individual backbench MSP).

One problem with the tax-varying power which was identified in the debate prior to introduction of the Scotland Bill was that, as it was linked to the basic rate of tax, the extent of the tax-varying flexibility open to the Scottish Parliament would be dependent on the UK tax structure. If, for example, the tax banding system used for income tax were to change, the potential of the tax-varying power would also change as a result, as can be seen from the change to the tax bands proposed in the 1999 Budget. Given that there has been a move in recent years to extend the impact of the lower rate taxation band, together with debate about more substantial tax reforms, it was felt by many commentators that the tax-varying powers of the Scottish Parliament should be flexible enough to cope with that eventuality. Section 76 of the SA 1998 attempts to deal with these concerns. It provides that if a proposed change to the income tax structure is such as to 'have a significant effect on the practical extent ... of the Parliament's tax-varying powers', the UK Treasury is required to put a statement before the House of Commons as to whether in its opinion a consequential variation of those tax-varying powers is required, and if so to make proposals for amending those powers accordingly. Any such proposal must be restricted to income tax (maintaining the exemption for income from savings and distributions), and any such amendment must be to the general effect that the tax-varying powers should remain 'broadly the same' as if it had been in force in 1997–98. In addition, any

---

[11] So sole traders and partners in firms would be liable to pay the varied rate of tax, but 'non-natural persons' will not.

[12] Amongst the types of income that *will* normally be covered are wages and salaries from employment, most pensions, the profits of a trade or profession, and the profits from land.

such amendment must not result in a 'significant difference' to the after-tax income of Scottish taxpayers.

Although the provisions for the use of the tax-varying power are comprehensively set out in the SA 1998, it remains to be seen what practical use will be made of those powers. If the block grant remains at current levels, the impact of the tax-varying power even if fully utilised will be minimal by comparison. In the White Paper, *Scotland's Parliament*, the Government considered[13] that the sum which would be raised in Scotland by increasing the basic rate of tax by 3p would be £450m. (This figure increased to £690m as a result of the change to tax bands in the 1999 Budget. By the 2003–04 tax year, as a result of the combined effect of changes in tax bands along with the effects of inflation and increases in tax yield, the estimate of the sum that would be raised by full use of the tax-varying power had increased to £840m.) This represents about 5% of the total funding provided by the block grant, which puts its significance into proportion.

Moreover, there would be costs incurred in setting up the system to vary income tax. In the White Paper, *Scotland's Parliament*, the government estimated that the cost to government and employers combined in setting up the necessary system to vary the basic rate tax would initially be in the region of £60m, and that the running costs thereafter would be between £14 and £23m per year (others have suggested that the costs might be higher). Given the relatively high cost of collection of the extra tax set against its potential yield (particularly if the power to vary taxes was not to be utilised to its full extent), it may be that there will be some reluctance amongst the Scottish political parties to use these powers. The Scottish Labour Party has stated that it will not use the tax-varying powers, at least in the initial years of the Parliament and that commitment was incorporated into the agreement between the Scottish Labour and Liberal Democrat parties establishing the coalition government after the first elections to the Parliament. In its election manifesto for those elections, the SNP restricted itself to a proposed use of the tax-raising power to the extent of a one penny increase only. By the time of the 2003 Scottish General Election the SNP had also dropped the commitment to use the power to increase taxes even to that limited extent. Accordingly, there certainly seems to be little prospect of the tax-varying power being used to increase taxes in the early years of the Parliament. There has been some debate about the possibility of using the power to reduce income tax in Scotland, but this too seems to be unlikely to occur, at least in the near future.

LOCAL TAXATION AND THE PARLIAMENT

It was mentioned above that the taxes and excise duties were matters which were generally reserved to the UK Parliament. That is why the SA 1998 has to give specific powers to the Scottish Parliament to have the tax-varying power described above. However, the Act does make clear that notwithstanding this general reservation of taxation, the Scottish Parliament will be able to legislate to make changes, if it so wishes, to the system of local taxation to fund local authority expenditure[14]. Council tax and non-domestic rates are given as specific examples of such local taxation on which the Parliament will be able to legislate.

---

[13] Paragraph 7.13.
[14] SA 1998, Sch 5, Pt II, s A1.

The Parliament has therefore been given broad powers to reform local taxation if it so wishes. It can make changes to the way that the present system is administered, for example, by changing the banding system for council tax. It could decide whether to retain the ability to set a level for the non-domestic rate (the 'business rate') on a Scotland-wide basis, or to leave local councils to determine its level. If it retains the ability to fix the business rate, it could decide the level at which it should be fixed. The Parliament can also decide whether to impose any 'cap' on the spending of local councils. The Parliament can also introduce fundamental reforms to the system of local government finance (e g funding local government by a land tax, or the introduction of a *local* tourist tax). It is suggested that the new forms of local taxation which could be introduced by the Parliament might even include a local sales tax, or indeed local income tax, although in practice such changes could probably only be brought about with the consent of the UK Parliament, as they would probably only be practicable if the UK sales and income taxes systems were modified to make the collection of such a tax possible. (It can be expected that any attempt to set up systems for collection of local sales taxes or income taxes which were separate from the UK VAT and income tax systems would be inordinately expensive and constitute an unwanted administrative burden for Scottish business. A local sales tax might conflict with EC rules.) Notwithstanding the powers available to it, however, no changes to the system of local taxation were made during the first term of the Scottish Parliament (1999–2003). However, the new programme for government[15] agreed by the Labour and Liberal Democrat parties when they negotiated a continuation of their governing coalition after the 2003 elections does include a commitment to establish an independent review into local government finance, which might result in recommendations for changes to the system of local taxation. The Scottish Executive has also retained the Scotland-wide uniform business rate, although it did introduce in 2003 a small business rate relief scheme which provided for reductions in rates paid by smaller businesses, funded by increases in rates for larger businesses.

As a substantial proportion of the finance provided by the block grant is then passed on to local government to support the services that it provides, the theoretical possibility exists that, even with the restricted tax-varying powers available to it, the Scottish Parliament could increase the real resources available to it by the device of reducing the sums it pays to local government. As a result, it would be able to retain a bigger share of the block grant, and local councils would have to meet the shortfall in resources either by cutting services or increasing local taxation. By such means, the Scottish Parliament could in effect increase its tax-raising powers by making use in an indirect manner of the taxation powers available to local government. However, although there are no specific provisions in the SA 1998 to meet such an eventuality, the government clearly had in mind when it launched its proposals for Scottish devolution that some controls over local government expenditure might be required. Consequently, it is stated in *Scotland's Parliament*[16] that if there were to be growth in the 'self-financed' expenditure of local councils which could be considered 'excessive and were such as to threaten targets set for public expenditure as management of the UK

---

[15] *A Partnership for a Better Scotland.* The text of the agreement can be found at www.scotland.gov.uk/library5/government/pfbs-00.asp.

[16] Paragraph 7.24.

economy ... it would be open to the UK Government to take the excess into account in considering the level of their support for expenditure in Scotland' if the Scottish Parliament chose not to take steps to reduce that growth in expenditure. In blunt terms, that would mean that if local councils increased local taxes, either because of their own decisions or as a result of reduction in grant support from the Scottish Parliament, the UK Government might well reduce the block grant payable to the Parliament. Such a threat would presumably serve as a powerful incentive (as was no doubt intended) to encourage the Scottish Parliament to restrain local government expenditure.

The activities of local government could have an indirect effect on the financial arrangements for a devolved Scotland in another way. At present, central government provides the bulk of the funding for the payments made by local councils as council tax and housing benefit. Under present arrangements, if local councils in Scotland were substantially to increase their levels of council tax and/or housing rent, the effect would be to increase the level of funding from central government. *Scotland's Parliament* makes it clear that the resources for these benefits will be included, after devolution, within the block grant, so that if expenditure on these benefits increases as a result of decisions taken by Scottish local councils, it will be the Scottish Parliament that will have to find the extra money[17].

It should be noted that, although there are potential mechanisms to allow the UK Government to recoup any additional expenditure incurred by it as an indirect result of actions by the Scottish Executive or local authorities in Scotland, there are no mechanisms (other than through negotiating an increase in block grant) to reimburse funds to the Scottish Executive if the UK Government saves money as a result of a decision by the Scottish Executive. This apparent imbalance was highlighted in 2001 when the Scottish Executive decided to fund free personal care for the elderly in Scotland. The Scottish Executive argued that as a result the UK Government would need to spend £23m less on social security payments in Scotland, and asked the UK Government to transfer that sum of money to the Scottish Executive to help it meet the cost of providing free personal care. The UK Government refused to give the Scottish Executive the additional funds, requiring the Scottish Executive to meet the additional cost from within the block grant it receives from the UK Government (which, admittedly, would begin to increase substantially at the time that the new costs for personal care would be incurred).

OTHER SOURCES OF FINANCE

The SA 1998 places no general restrictions on the Scottish Parliament from introducing charges for services provided by the Scottish Administration, or which other bodies provide on its behalf. Accordingly, it has the power to raise finance in such a way as long as the activity to be supported is one which falls within its general remit. If the level of charge made, however, was such as to raise income in excess of the cost of the provision of the service, it is suggested that the excess amount of the charge might well be regarded as in reality a tax, which would therefore be beyond the powers of the Scottish Parliament to impose (unless it were to fall within the definition of local taxation).

---

[17] Paragraph 7.25.

One source of funding which is becoming of increasing importance in a number of areas of government activity which in general fall within the remit of the Scottish Parliament is the National Lottery. 'Betting, gaming and lotteries' is a matter reserved to the UK Parliament[18], so the Scottish Parliament and Executive cannot legislate to establish a Scottish lottery or have any statutory right to be involved in the management or the disbursement of funds raised by the National Lottery. However, one of the Concordats between the Scottish Executive and the UK Government provided for the Scottish Ministers to be given certain powers to make directions and be consulted on appointments to other Lottery distribution bodies[19]. It also provided that the Annual Reports and Accounts of all the Scottish and UK Lottery distributors except the Millennium Commission, and the Annual Report of the National Lottery Commission, are to be laid before the Scottish Parliament as well as the UK Parliament.

As a result of the implementation of that Concordat, the Scottish Executive can issue policy directions to the Scottish Arts and Council and sportscotland, subject to consultation with the UK Secretary of State. It can also issue policy directions to UK-wide distributors in as much as they impinge on devolved matters, subject in this case to the agreement of the UK Secretary of State. Although the Scottish Executive cannot vary Scotland's share of the total funds raised by the Lottery, it does therefore have powers to ensure that the substantial funds available to the lottery distribution bodies are allocated within Scotland in such a way as to reflect its general policy priorities. Following a consultation exercise, the UK Secretary of State for Culture, Media and Sport announced in 2003 that she proposed to give the devolved administrations in Scotland, Wales and Northern Ireland 'more direct influence' over how Lottery money is spent in their countries, although a UK-wide structure for distribution would be retained[20].

As there are no specific reservations in the SA 1998 preventing the Scottish Executive from obtaining grant aid for its activities, there is presumably no reason why it should not also seek grants from any source that might be prepared to finance its activities.

THE COSTS OF THE PARLIAMENT'S NEW BUILDING

Finally, mention should also be made of the costs of the Scottish Parliament's new permanent building at Holyrood. During the Scottish Parliament's first term, and into its second, the rising cost of this project was probably the one issue of public expenditure related to the new constitutional arrangements which attracted the most public attention. In July 1997, the UK Government stated in the White Paper, *Scotland's Parliament*[21] that the cost of providing a building for the Parliament would be between £10 and £40m. However, by June 2003, the cost of the (still uncompleted) building had risen to £375m. Some commentators suggested that by the time that the new building was eventually completed,

---

[18] SA 1998, Sch 5, Pt II, s B9.

[19] *Concordat between Department for Culture, Media and Sport and the Scottish Executive*, http://www.scotland.gov.uk/concordats/dcms-06.asp.

[20] See Department of Culture, Media and Sport *National Lottery Funding: Decision Document* (July 2003) paras 4.20–4.22.

[21] Paragraph 10.7. It was stated that the building might be either a new building or a conversion of an existing building.

probably in 2004, the final cost might have risen to more than £400m. During the 2003 General Election campaign, the First Minister announced he intended to set up an independent inquiry into the costs of the Holyrood building. This inquiry was set up in June 2003, headed by the former Lord Advocate and Conservative Scottish Office Minister, Lord Fraser of Carmyllie. In addition, the Auditor General was invited to examine any issues of financial probity arising out of the matter[22].

---

[22] See www.scotland.gov.uk/pages/news/2003/06/SENW543.aspx.

10 THE PARLIAMENT, LOCAL GOVERNMENT AND OTHER PUBLIC BODIES

INTRODUCTION

The relationship between the Parliament and local government deserves special attention as both are tiers of government, elected by a wide popular franchise, accountable through the ballot box and with tax-raising powers. While doing its preparatory work for a Scottish Parliament, the Scottish Constitutional Convention always envisaged that local government would be one of the matters devolved to the Parliament. In its final report, *Scotland's Parliament: Scotland's Right*[1], the SCC recommended that:

- the relationship between the Parliament and local government should be positive, co-operative and stable;
- the principles of the European Charter of Local Self-Government should be adopted, in particular Art 4 which provides that local authorities should, within the limits of the law, have full discretion to exercise their initiative with regard to any matter which is not excluded from their competence nor assigned to any other authority;
- any future review of Scottish local government should adopt the following aims:
  (a) to safeguard and where possible increase local authority discretion;
  (b) to ensure that proposals for reform are widely acceptable in Scotland;
  (c) to ensure a system of local government finance which sustains local accountability[2].

Finally, it recommended that the Scotland Act 1998 (SA 1998) should contain a section committing the Parliament to securing and maintaining a strong and effective system of local government, embodying the principle of subsidiarity as a guarantee of local government in service delivery.

The White Paper, *Scotland's Parliament*, contained a short chapter on local government and other bodies[3]. It laid out the following general principles:

- the government does not expect the Scottish Parliament to accumulate a range of new functions at the centre which would be more appropriately and efficiently delivered by other bodies within Scotland;
- decisions should be made as close as possible to the citizens of Scotland (the principle of subsidiarity);

---

[1] pp 16–17.

[2] At present, local government raises only approximately 20% of its income through the council tax. The remainder is financed by the Scottish Executive. See pp 120–21.

[3] Chapter 6.

- the Scottish Parliament should set the national framework within which other Scottish public bodies operate.

On local government in particular, the White Paper made it clear that the Scottish Parliament has general responsibility for legislation and policy relating to local government. It has the power to set the framework within which local government operates and to make changes to its powers, boundaries and functions. The Scottish Executive has responsibility for local government expenditure and for the system of local taxation.

The SA 1998 is virtually silent about the matter of local government but, as has already been discussed, the government opted for the retaining model for the legislation[4] and the only references to local government in Sch 5[5] (which covers reserved matters) are to:

- local taxes (which are excepted from reservation); and
- the franchise at local government elections (which is reserved).

It would seem, therefore, that all other aspects of local government are devolved to the Scottish Parliament. However, some of the functions of local government, such as weights and measures, housing benefit, the treatment of asylum seekers and the control of fireworks, relate to matters which are reserved. The way in which the SA 1998 deals with this is to define local authorities as 'Scottish public authorities with mixed functions'[6]. This ensures that local authorities and the majority of their functions remain devolved, while functions which relate to reserved matters remain reserved.

Leaving aside the reserved functions, the Parliament is able to pass legislation on any aspect of local government. It could change the boundaries and the structure completely, although the Scottish Executive made it clear in 2002 that it did not plan to review council boundaries (because of the disruption to the public and to local government employees which a reorganisation entails) or to reduce the number of Scottish councillors in the foreseeable future. The Parliament could add functions to, or take functions from, local government and change the way in which services are delivered and how local government is managed. It has responsibility for the financing of local government, both through the system of grants and through determining the form of local taxation.

Scottish Ministers have wide powers to scrutinise the activities of local government either through inspectorates or through bodies such as the Accounts Commission and the Standards Commission. They have powers to regulate the activities of local government by requiring local authorities to maintain certain standards in, for example, education, social work, law and order. There are also some powers of intervention.

The relationship between the Scottish Parliament and local government is, however, not statutorily defined, despite the recommendation of the Scottish Constitutional Convention, and fears have been expressed by many people working in local government as officers and members that the Scottish Parliament will suck up the powers of local government to itself.

---

[4] See ch 3.
[5] Schedule 5 covers the matters reserved to the UK Parliament.
[6] SA 1998, Sch 5, Pt III.

THE STRUCTURE AND FUNCTIONS OF LOCAL GOVERNMENT

Before examining the relationship between the Scottish Parliament and local government, it is necessary to give a brief description of the current structure and functions of local government in Scotland. This will make clear the reasons for the fears mentioned above.

Between 1975 and 1996, local government on mainland Scotland was organised on a two-tier basis with 9 regional and 53 district councils. There were also three islands councils. The regional councils ranged in population from 2.3 million in Strathclyde Region to 103,000 in the Borders region[7]. The regional councils were responsible for those local government functions which required a relatively large geographical or population base. These included education, police and fire services, social work, roads and transportation, water and sewerage and a number of others including consumer protection.

The district councils ranged in population from 689,000 in Glasgow District to 10,420 in Nairn District. The district councils were responsible for the more local services such as local planning and development control, libraries, museums, parks, refuse collection and disposal, cleansing and environmental health and a wide range of licensing and other regulatory functions. By far the most important and costly district function was housing. Because of the sparsity of population in some rural areas, the district councils lying within the Highlands, the Borders and Dumfries and Galloway Regions did not have responsibility for libraries, building control and local planning. Instead these were carried out by the regional councils.

The islands councils for Orkney, Shetland and the Western Isles were treated as special cases and, despite their small populations, were given single-tier most-purpose status. They were responsible for the delivery of virtually all the local government functions with the exception of police and fire which they shared with Highland Regional Council.

The two-tier system of local government was in existence during the discussions on Scottish devolution in the 1970s which culminated in the Scotland Act 1978. That Act was to have established a Scottish Assembly with legislative powers but no powers to raise tax. One of the arguments against devolution at that time was that the establishment of a Scottish Assembly, in addition to the two-tier system of local government, the UK Parliament and the European Parliament (plus community councils in many areas) would lead to Scotland being over-governed. In political terms, it was difficult to envisage how Strathclyde Regional Council, large and powerful, covering more than half the population of Scotland, with an annual budget of around £2.2bn and local tax-raising powers, could co-exist amicably with a Scottish Assembly which did not have the power to raise even a penny on its own. The Scottish Assembly, however, was never established as the threshold in the referendum of March 1979 of 40 per cent of the electorate voting 'Yes' was not reached[8]. The Conservative Government which was elected in May 1979 repealed the Scotland Act 1978 later that year.

---

[7] 1990 figures.
[8] See ch 1.

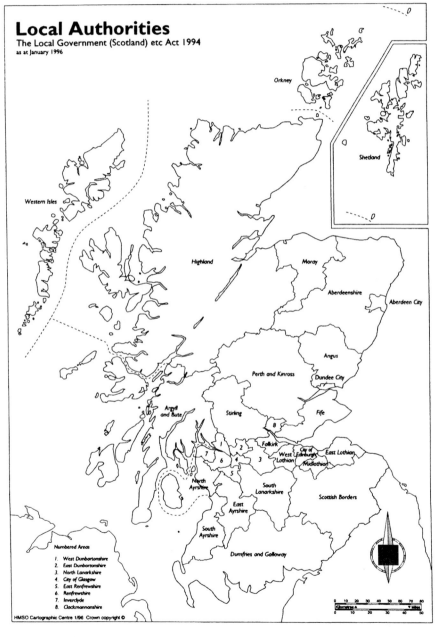

Local Authorities

The Local Government (Scotland) etc Act 1994
as at January 1996

Crown copyright is reproduced with the permission of the Controller of Her Majesty's
Stationery Office.

LOCAL GOVERNMENT REORGANISATION

In 1991 the Conservative Government announced, somewhat unexpectedly, that it intended to reorganise Scottish local government by abolishing the two-tier system and replacing it with single-tier authorities. In a consultation paper, *The Case for Change*, it was argued that the two-tier system was not readily understood by the public, that it led to a clouding of accountability, and that some of the regions were seen as too large and too remote[9]. It was also argued that the system resulted *inevitably* in duplication, waste, delays and friction between the two tiers. The case for a single-tier system was basically the mirror image of the criticisms of the two-tier system. It was asserted that it was simple to understand and therefore clarified accountability and that it removed the potential for duplication, waste, delay and friction between the two tiers[10].

The government's proposals were not welcomed with any enthusiasm in Scotland, least of all by those involved in local government, but the government pressed ahead and passed the Local Government etc (Scotland) Act 1994 (LG(S)A 1994). The regional and district councils were abolished on 30 March 1996 and were replaced by 29 single-tier councils on mainland Scotland[11]. The three island councils which had been virtually all-purpose remained unchanged. The 29 new councils came into existence on 1 April 1996 following a 'shadow' year during which they co-existed with the regional and district councils. They ranged in terms of population from Glasgow City Council with 618,430 to Clackmannanshire Council with 48,810. Twelve of the new councils had populations of fewer than 100,000. As a result of the small populations of some of the councils, it was not feasible to transfer the entire range of local authority functions to each of the 29 new councils. A council with a population of less than 100,000 is not able to provide, for example, police and fire services on a cost-effective basis. As a result, arrangements were made in the Act for some functions to be removed from local government altogether and for others to be handled on a joint basis by a consortium of councils.

The functions which were removed from local government are:

- water and sewerage – transferred initially to three Water and Sewerage Authorities whose members were appointed by the Secretary of State for Scotland; in 2002 a single Water Authority was established to take the place of the three authorities. Its members are appointed by the Scottish Ministers[12];
- the children's reporter system – transferred to the Scottish Children's Reporters Administration whose members were appointed by the Secretary of State for Scotland (now by Scottish Ministers).

The functions handled jointly are:

- police – eight police forces established, six of which are run by joint boards, consisting of representatives of three or more of the new councils. Fife Council has its own police force as does Dumfries and

---

[9] *The Structure of Local Government: The Case for Change* paras 9–10.
[10] *The Structure of Local Government: The Case for Change* paras 16–17.
[11] See map on p 111.
[12] Water Industry (Scotland) Act 2002.

Galloway Council. In the case of Strathclyde Police Force no fewer than 12 councils are involved in the joint board;

- fire services – eight fire brigades established on a basis similar to that for the police forces described above;
- property valuation for council tax and non-domestic rates purposes – run by 10 joint boards. Dumfries and Galloway, Fife, Glasgow, Dundee, and the Scottish Borders Councils are the only councils not involved in joint arrangements;
- structure planning – 17 structure plan areas established, many of which are run by joint committees;
- public transport – a Strathclyde Passenger Authority established to run public transport in most of the areas of Strathclyde.

Because of the small size of some of the councils, it has been necessary for them to enter into joint arrangements or agency agreements with their neighbours to provide specialist services in, for example, education and social work. A survey carried out by the Convention of Scottish Local Authorities (COSLA) found that between 1996 and 1998 a total of 333 voluntary joint arrangements had been established by Scotland's councils[13].

Joint committees, boards and other arrangements are not new. There was widespread use of them in Scotland before the introduction of the two-tier system in 1975, when there was a cumbersome structure of over 400 local authorities. Joint arrangements, however, have their drawbacks and have been described as notoriously ineffective. The smaller councils tend to feel dominated by their larger colleagues, they tend to be officer-led rather than member-led and, since their members are appointed by the councils and are not directly elected, they lack democratic legitimacy and direct accountability to the electorate.

THE RELATIONSHIP BETWEEN THE SCOTTISH PARLIAMENT AND LOCAL GOVERNMENT

Because of the fragmented nature of local government and the plethora of joint arrangements which now exist, some local government members and officers see the establishment of the Scottish Parliament as a threat. They see it as an institution which will further undermine local autonomy. Since certain important services are now carried out under joint boards or committees, the accountability of which is diluted, might the Scottish Parliament, itself directly elected, take control of these services? From time to time there is discussion of a national police force and a national fire service. Structure planning too might be carried out on a Scotland-wide basis. Although it is unlikely that the Scottish Parliament or Executive would want to take direct control of all Scottish schools or the entire social work service[14], the Parliament certainly has the power to make educational and social work policies and set standards. Will these policies and standards be drawn so tightly that local discretion is removed and the local authorities become little more than agents of the Scottish Parliament? There was also the fear that the Parliament, with 129 MSPs, would not provide enough Parliamentary work to keep all its members busy and therefore those without ministerial office might feel

---

[13] COSLA: Voluntary Joint Working Arrangements by Councils 1996/7 and 1997/8.
[14] See pp 124–25 for the Scottish Executive's proposed incursions into these areas.

tempted to interfere in the administration of local government functions. This fear has proved, to some extent, to be unfounded as the committee work of the Parliament keeps the MSPs busy. However, many of them take up local government issues on behalf of their constituents, often to the annoyance of their councillor colleagues. Others take a more optimistic view and see the establishment of the Parliament as an opportunity for a fresh start in which two democratically elected institutions can work in partnership, with local government contributing to the development and monitoring of policies.

There has been discussion of the possibility of a concordat, a document which would set out and regulate the relationship between the Parliament and local government. Some see this as a document with the force of law, entrenching the autonomy of local government and preventing the Parliament from encroaching on the traditional powers and functions of councils. Others take the view that the Parliament, which has statutory responsibility for all aspects of local government, except the franchise, cannot be prevented from making changes to the framework within which local government operates, as and when circumstances dictate. A concordat could, however, set out a political commitment to the principle of subsidiarity. The UK Government gave an indication of their commitment to local government by signing and ratifying the European Charter of Local Self-Government shortly after taking office in 1997.

THE McINTOSH COMMISSION

Partly in response to the fears expressed above and prior to the passing of the SA 1998, the Secretary of State for Scotland established a Commission on Local Government and the Scottish Parliament. The Commission was chaired by Neil McIntosh who was the last Chief Executive of Strathclyde Regional Council prior to its abolition in 1996.

Its remit was:

- to consider how to build the most effective relations between local government and the Scottish Parliament and Scottish Executive; and
- to consider how councils can best make themselves responsive and democratically accountable to the communities they serve.

The Commission carried out extensive consultations with interested bodies and presented its final report to the First Minister of the Scottish Executive in June 1999.

Two consultation papers were issued. The first invited comments as to how the relationship between local government (both collectively and at the level of the individual council) and the Scottish Parliament and the Scottish Executive should be established. The second consultation paper commented on responses made to the first paper and posed a series of further questions for consideration. As McIntosh pointed out[15], it is important to understand the nature of any partnership between central and local government, so that any expectations of that partnership are realistic. Local government is the creature of statute. It is brought into being by an Act of Parliament and can just as easily be abolished by an Act of

---

[15] Consultation Paper 2, p 8.

Parliament. The power to legislate on local government has been devolved to the Scottish Parliament. So the partnership between local government and the Scottish Parliament can never be one of equals since the Parliament ultimately holds power over local government. Nevertheless, it would stand on its head the principle of subsidiarity (ie that decisions should be taken as closely as possible to those whom they affect) if the Scottish Parliament and Executive were to concentrate the powers traditionally exercised by local government in their own hands. If local government is to be strong and effective as both the Scottish Constitutional Convention and the Government in the White Paper recommended, central government in Edinburgh should not dominate local government.

The report of the Commission

The McIntosh Commission Report on Local Government and the Scottish Parliament was published in June 1999, the month following the first election to the Scottish Parliament[16]. Somewhat surprisingly, the actual relationship between the Scottish Parliament and local government was dealt with in only eight pages. The remainder dealt with various other local government issues including the method of election to local councils, the conduct of council business and community councils.

The relationship between the Scottish Parliament and local government

The Commission recognised that the establishment of the Parliament represented a fundamental change in the political landscape in which councils operate. Although each has a democratic base, it is the Parliament which has the ultimate power to determine what becomes of local government.

It believed that the principle of subsidiarity should be the key. That principle underlies the SA 1998 which created the Parliament and should be equally applicable to the relationship between the Parliament and local government. If a greater centralisation of power is proposed, the onus of proof should be on those who propose centralisation to demonstrate that it will bring greater benefit to the public at large. Since both have a common democratic basis, relations between local government and the Parliament should be on the basis of mutual respect and parity of esteem.

However, McIntosh asserted that if local government were to earn that parity of esteem, the Parliament would have to be convinced that it is dealing with local authorities which are as responsive to and as representative of their electorates as possible and which are ready and willing to embrace renewal in their attitudes and working practices. Certain principles drawn from those laid down for the Parliament are set out:

- accountability;
- accessibility, transparency, responsiveness and a participative approach;
- equal opportunities for all.

---

[16] Report of the Commission on Local Government and the Scottish Parliament *Moving Forward: Local Government and the Scottish Parliament*. (the McIntosh Report) (June 1999).

These are further developed into:

- participation by the citizen;
- transparency in the conduct of council business;
- focus on the customer;
- delivery of quality and cost-effective services;
- partnership working;
- improvement of the public image;
- promotion of active citizenship and social inclusion;
- good employment practices.

Although many of these are to be found in local government at present, McIntosh warned that if local government does not deliver to the Parliament's satisfaction, the Parliament would look elsewhere – perhaps to quangos, accountable to Ministers and local government will find itself progressively stripped of functions and influence.

The covenant and the Joint Conference

The Report called for the Parliament and the councils to commit themselves to a concordat or covenant, setting out the basis of their working relationship, and to set up a standing Joint Conference where MSPs and council representatives could hold a dialogue on the basis of equality[17]. A draft covenant is included as an appendix to the Report, containing the following general principles:

- respect for each other's roles;
- partnership on strategic issues;
- genuine consultation prior to any major restructuring of local government;
- pre-legislative discussion on local government issues;
- a sound financial base for local government;
- the principle of subsidiarity;
- openness and accountability;
- a recognition of councils' key roles in service provision and as co-ordinators of service delivery.

The covenant should not be enforced through the courts nor by any other formal mechanism but by the political necessity of keeping to it. However, the Joint Conference should monitor its application and consider modifications from time to time.

It was suggested that the Joint Conference should consist of not more than 15 representatives each of the Parliament (not Ministers) and of local government. The chairmanship [sic] should alternate annually between the parliamentary and the local government sides. It should meet regularly and local government policy issues should be able to be placed on the agenda by either side. Any local authority or MSP should have the right to submit papers on agenda items. Scottish Ministers may be invited and should be entitled to attend and speak. At least once

---

[17] The McIntosh Report, para 34.

a year all council leaders should be invited to attend. The Conference should work towards improved public service standards, provide an opportunity for the exchange of ideas, review policy and consider legislative proposals. It should produce an annual 'State of Local Government' report.

Unfortunately, these recommendations have yet to be implemented. There was already in existence, prior to the establishment of the Parliament, a formal working agreement between the Convention of Scottish Local Authorities (COSLA) and the Scottish Office. McIntosh recommends that a similar agreement should be established between local government and the Scottish Ministers[18]. A draft is included as an appendix to the Report. The general principles are almost identical to those suggested for the covenant. In addition, it suggests that the Scottish Ministers should commit themselves to consultation with COSLA, as the representative body of local authorities in Scotland, on policy issues affecting local government. COSLA should also be consulted during the pre-legislative phase on legislative proposals affecting local government. Sufficient time should be allowed, where possible, for a considered and representative response. Scottish Ministers should always convey public announcements directly concerning local government to COSLA no later than to the media and, where possible, in advance. COSLA should reciprocate in relation to announcements concerning Scottish Ministers. The First Minister and the Scottish Ministers responsible for major services should meet COSLA on a regular basis to exchange views. Either side should be able to request ad hoc meetings to discuss a specific subject. COSLA should be consulted on the appointment of local government representatives to other bodies.

The Commission's recommendations on local authority powers

It is a well-established principle of law that a statutory body has no power to do anything which it is not authorised or required to do by the statute or statutes under which the body was constituted or which otherwise govern its activities. This is the ultra vires rule. In many other countries local governments may do anything for the benefit of their communities which is not specifically reserved or prohibited or provided for through other legislation. Such a power is generally referred to as a power of general competence.

The McIntosh Commission recognised that legislation giving local government a power of general competence would require careful drafting but nevertheless saw significant benefits in providing such a power and recommended that such a statutory power should be introduced[19]. The Commission saw the benefits of such a power to include:

- giving specific statutory form to the principle of subsidiarity on a parallel with the SA 1998 itself which empowers the Scottish Parliament to do whatever is not specifically reserved to Westminster;
- giving statutory expression to the unwritten purpose of a local council, namely to be the voice of its people and promote their interests;
- facilitating the process of community planning by increasing the freedom of councils to take part in joint action with other agencies.

---

[18] The McIntosh Report, para 45.
[19] The McIntosh Report, para 50.

Miscellaneous recommendations of the McIntosh Commission

The second leg of the McIntosh Commission's remit was to consider how councils might best make themselves responsive and democratically accountable to the communities they serve. The Commission interpreted this broadly and made a series of wide-ranging recommendations. These included[20]:

- the simplification of the rules and procedures for the conduct of local government elections;
- the reintroduction of a four-year term for councils;
- a system of proportional representation for the election of councils;
- changes to the way in which local government business is organised;
- a pay and conditions package for councillors;
- a relaxation of the rule which prevents local government employees from standing for election to the council which employs them;
- a statutory power of general competence for councils;
- the immediate institution of an independent inquiry into local government finance.

The response of the Scottish Executive to the report of the McIntosh Commission

Very soon after the publication of the McIntosh Report, the Scottish Executive, in a ministerial statement, announced acceptance of the majority of the Commission's recommendations and the establishment of a cross-party working party to examine, inter alia, widening access to council membership, electoral reform and the remuneration of councillors[21]. The Scottish Executive announced at the same time that all councils were to undertake a review of organisational structures and, in August 1999, an advisory panel was established to advise councils on their reviews[22]. The statement also included an indication of support for a four-year term for councils.

The Scottish Executive published a fuller response and a consultation paper on various other issues raised by the Report of the Commission in September 1999[23]. The issues on which views were invited included:

- a power of general competence;
- the timing of local elections[24];
- directly elected council leaders[25];
- election of council employees to their own council and politically restricted posts.

---

[20] The McIntosh Report, para 66.

[21] The working party was chaired by Richard Kerley of Edinburgh University and became known as the Renewing Local Democracy Group. It reported in June 2000.

[22] The panel was chaired by Alistair McNish, a former local government chief executive, and became known as the Leadership Advisory Panel. It reported in April 2000.

[23] Scottish Executive *Report of the Commission on Local Government and the Scottish Parliament: The Scottish Executive's Response* (September 1999).

[24] Ie whether local elections should be held on the same day as Scottish Parliamentary elections or mid term.

[25] On the model of the directly elected Mayor of the Greater London Authority, provided for in the Greater London Authority Act 1999 (see ch 12).

The Scottish Executive, however, made it clear that they were not persuaded of the need for an independent review of local government finance. The consultation paper made no mention of the covenant or the Joint Conference.

The ministerial statement and the fuller response and consultation paper, issued so early in the life of the Scottish Parliament, gave a clear indication that the Scottish Executive and the Parliament were acutely aware of the importance of local government and of the need for legislative change in a large number of areas. Local government members and officers alike generally welcomed the more positive attitude which contrasted starkly with the attitude of central government to local government during the 1980s and 1990s, prior to devolution.

Report of the Renewing Local Democracy Working Group (the Kerley Report)

The Renewing Local Democracy Working Group set up to examine widening access to council membership, electoral reform and the remuneration of councillors produced its report in June 2000. Its recommendations included[26]:

- a package of proposals designed to widen access to council membership, in particular, the reduction of the minimum age for standing for election from 21 years to 18[27];
- a revised and improved system of remuneration for councillors;
- the introduction of a system of proportional representation for local government elections, the preferred system being the single transferable vote;
- a reduction in the number of councillors per council to a maximum of 53, with the exception of Highland Council which might have up to a maximum of 63 to reflect the exceptional travelling demands on councillors in the Highlands.

Report of the Leadership Advisory Panel (the McNish Report)

The Scottish Executive has not been prescriptive in its attitude to local government organisational and decision-making structures. This is in contrast to the position in England and Wales where the Local Government Act 2000 requires most councils to choose one of the following executive arrangements:

- an elected mayor and executive;
- an appointed leader and executive; or
- an elected mayor and council manager.

Only councils with a population under 85,000 may opt for a reformed committee structure.

When the Scottish Executive announced the establishment of the Leadership Advisory Panel to advise councils on their reviews of their organisational and decision-making structures, the following criteria were laid down:

---

[26] The Kerley Report, chs 3–6.
[27] The current age for standing for election (ie 21) is set out in the Local Government (Scotland) Act 1973, s 29(1).

- openness in decision making;
- effective scrutiny of the acts of the leadership;
- transparency in the use of the whip;
- the organisation of council business to allow a wider cross-section of the public to consider becoming councillors.

The Panel reported in April 2001.

The bulk of the report is made up of a review, council by council, of proposals for change, tested against the panel's criteria. By April 2001, all but three Scottish councils[28] had undertaken reviews of their decision-making structures. Three general categories of structures emerged:

- streamlined committee structures
- executives
- devolved and partially devolved structures.

Although critical of a small number of councils, the panel's evaluation of the 32 councils' submissions was generally positive. Its conclusions were:

- the majority of councils had engaged proactively in the review process;
- real progress had been made in reducing bureaucracy;
- the formal executive model works well if a genuine scrutiny role is provided for the non-executive members;
- streamlined committee structures must provide a significant scrutiny role for backbench councillors;
- most councils are comfortable with announcing which items of business are 'whipped'

Scottish local authorities welcomed the lightness of touch in the Scottish Executive's attitude towards the organisation of local government business and decision making as compared with the position in England and Wales.

Local Government Committee of the Scottish Parliament

As we have seen, one of the strengths of the Scottish Parliament is its committee system (see ch 4). A Local Government Committee was established early in the life of the Parliament and its first convener was a former councillor as were many of its initial members. The remit of the Committee is to consider and report on matters relating to local government, including local government finance.

The Committee undertakes the committee stages of Bills relating to local government including the taking of evidence from interested parties on legislative proposals. An indication of the independence of the Committee from the Executive was its decision to undertake a comprehensive inquiry into local government finance, following the Scottish Executive's decision not to accept the McIntosh Commission's request for an independent inquiry. The inquiry was commenced in September 2000 and the Committee's Report was presented to the Scottish Parliament in March 2002. It strongly recommended that the

---

[28] Ie Aberdeenshire, Dundee City and South Ayrshire councils. Three other councils, ie Angus, Clackmannanshire and Shetland Islands, decided to make no changes to their existing structures.

central–local funding balance should change from the existing 80 per cent central, 20 per cent local split to a 50:50 split. Such a change would significantly lessen local government's dependence on central government and increase local accountability. However, the Scottish Executive rejected this proposal.

LOCAL GOVERNMENT LEGISLATION IN THE FIRST TERM OF THE SCOTTISH PARLIAMENT[29]

Ethical Standards in Public Life etc (Scotland) Act 2000

Prior to the election of the Scottish Parliament in 1999, the Scottish Office had been carrying out a consultation on standards of conduct in local government[30]. The Scottish Ministers, on appointment, found that a draft Bill had already been prepared and before the end of 1999 produced their own consultation paper and draft Bill on the issue[31]. The Ethical Standards in Public Life etc (Scotland) Act 2000 introduced for the first time a binding statutory code of conduct for local authority members (and a model code for members of relevant public bodies). The Act established a Standards Commission whose members are appointed by the Scottish Ministers and whose remit is to enforce compliance with the codes. The Commission is assisted by a Chief Investigating Officer whose function is to investigate and report on cases in which a councillor is alleged to have contravened the councillor's code. The penalties available to the Standards Commission in relation to councillors are censure, suspension from attendance at council and committee meetings for up to one year and disqualification from elected office for up to five years. During the passage of the Bill, the Scottish Executive decided to amend the Bill to abolish the penalty of personal surcharge against councillors and local government officers for financial irregularities[32].

The constitutional significance of this Act is threefold. First, it imposes a statutory code of conduct on local authority members. Second, it gives the power to disqualify councillors to an unelected public body, a power which previously lay with the electorate or, as a last resort, with the courts. Third, it repeals the controversial and unfair penalty of surcharge, replacing it (for councillors) with a process and penalties similar to those involving contravention of the code of conduct.

Scottish Local Government (Elections Act) 2002

The McIntosh Commission had recommended that the term of Scottish councils should be restored to four years from the three years provided for in s 5(3) of the LG(S)A 1994. The Scottish Executive consulted on this recommendation in its

---

[29] This section refers to what might broadly be called legislation of constitutional significance for local government. It does not deal with legislation relating to local government functions, such as education and housing.

[30] Scottish Office 'A New Ethical Framework for Local Government in Scotland' (1998).

[31] This Bill also contained the very controversial proposal to repeal s 2A of the Local Government Act 1986 which is better (though mistakenly) known as 'section 28'. This section prohibited local authorities from promoting homosexuality.

[32] The penalty of surcharge and the processes leading up to it were contained in the Local Government (Scotland) Act 1973, ss 102–104.

response to the Report of the Commission. Respondents were overwhelmingly in favour of a four-year term but divided as to whether the local government elections should be held on the same day as the Scottish Parliamentary elections or mid-term.

The Scottish Executive opted for the synchronisation of the elections. The Scottish Local Government (Elections) Act 2002 (SLG(E)A 2002) amends s 5(3) of the LG(S)A 1994 so that local government elections will be held on the day of the ordinary general election to the Scottish Parliament[33]. The term of the councils which were elected in 1999 and which should have come to an end in May 2002 was extended to 2003.

The SLG(E)A 2002 also gives local authorities the power, with the Scottish Ministers' consent, to pilot new electoral procedures. These procedures may include: changes in where and when local government elections are to take place; the method used to cast votes; how the votes are to be counted; the sending by candidates of election communications free of charge for postage; changes to any other matter relating to action to be taken, or procedure to be carried out, before or during the poll which would facilitate voting or encourage more people to vote. While local government members and officers welcomed the increased stability and the chance to plan more effectively provided by a four-year term, there were mixed feelings about the provision to hold local government elections on the same day as the Parliamentary elections. It is likely that synchronisation will increase the turnout at local government elections[34], but it is possible that the voters will be influenced more by national than by local government considerations in casting their votes. It is feared that this could reduce the accountability of local councillors to their electorates rather than enhance it. However, it is interesting to note that in the synchronised elections of 2003, in certain constituencies more votes were cast for the council candidates than for the candidates for the Scottish Parliament.

Local Government in Scotland Act 2003

The Local Government in Scotland Act 2003 (LGSA 2003) contained three major provisions and a number of miscellaneous minor provisions. The three main provisions are[35]:

- a duty on local authorities to secure best value;
- a duty on local authorities to initiate and maintain community planning;
- a power to advance well-being.

Best value is defined as continuous improvement in a local authority's functions, with an appropriate balance between the quality and the cost of the performance. Community planning is defined as a process by which a local authority, other public bodies and the local community come together to plan, provide and promote the well-being of their communities. The local authority has the lead

---

[33] The day of the ordinary general election to the Scottish Parliament is the first Thursday in May, every fourth year from 1999: SA 1998, s 2(2).

[34] The turnout at local government elections reached 50% on only one occasion between 1974 and 1996. In 1999, when the local government elections coincided with the first election to the Scottish Parliament, the turnout rose to 58.5%.

[35] LGSA 2003, Pts 1–3.

role, having a duty to initiate, maintain and facilitate the process. The power to advance well-being is a new discretionary power which enables local authorities to do anything they consider is likely to promote the well-being of their areas and/or persons in them. This power includes, inter alia the power to incur expenditure; to give financial assistance; to exercise on behalf of any person any function of that person; and to provide goods, services or accommodation. Detailed guidance has been issued on all three of these provisions by the Scottish Ministers and local authorities must have regard to the guidance.

In the case of the power to advance well-being, the McIntosh Commission had recommended that local government should be given a power of general competence and the Scottish Executive had consulted early on this issue. Most of the respondents to the Scottish Executive's various consultation papers were in favour of a power of general competence in some form or other as the ultra vires rule had caused major problems to local government and those with whom it works, over the years. For example, it was decided in *Morgan Guaranty Trust Company of New York v Lothian Regional Council*[36] that local authorities had no power to enter into interest rate swaps, a decision which, along with similar English decisions, had led to unwillingness on the part of financial institutions to deal with local authorities. As the Scottish Executive's thinking on this issue developed, the power was renamed 'a power of community initiative' and later, when the Bill was introduced, 'a power to advance well-being'.

The power to advance well-being does not abolish the ultra vires rule as it would be impossible to give a body established by statute what would amount to sovereignty. Nevertheless, the power significantly reduces the harshness of the rule. However, the LGSA 2003 gives control of the excess of the power to advance well-being initially to the Scottish Ministers. Whether the transfer of the control of the excess of the power from the courts to the Scottish Executive will be to the advantage of local government remains to be seen.

LOCAL GOVERNMENT AND THE SCOTTISH PARLIAMENT'S FIRST SESSION: AN EVALUATION

At the end of the first session of the Scottish Parliament, in March 2003, the fears of local government that the Scottish Parliament would take over powers of local authorities had proved to be largely unfounded. Several of the legislative changes which local government members and officers had been requesting over many years, such as the abolition of surcharge and something akin to a power of general competence in the form of the power to advance well-being, had found their way to the statute book. The four-year term for councils had been restored. The Scottish Executive had announced that there would be no enforced reduction in the number of councillors, had ruled out the upheaval of another reorganisation of local authority boundaries for the time being and was looking sympathetically at relaxing political restrictions on council employees. A commitment had been given to change the system of councillors' allowances and to establish some kind of pension provision. Consultation processes appeared to be fruitful in that the Scottish Executive was willing, on occasion, to introduce amendments to Bills during their process through the Parliament in response to issues raised by

---

[36] 1995 SCLR 225; 1995 SLT 215.

respondents[37]. The Scottish Executive's position regarding organisational and decision-making arrangements within individual councils had been less prescriptive than local government had feared.

On the negative side, there had been little progress in implementing the recommendations of the Commission on Local Government and the Scottish Parliament that a covenant should be agreed between the Scottish Parliament and the 32 local authorities and that a standing Joint Conference should be established.

A study on the impact of devolution on local government found that, with the Parliament and the Scottish Executive located in Edinburgh, Ministers and MSPs are far more accessible than were the Scottish Office Ministers in pre-devolution days and the general feeling in local government was that Ministers and civil servants are more open and responsive than in the past[38]. The views of councillors were mixed as to whether the Scottish Executive had diminished the importance of local government[39].

FUTURE PROSPECTS FOR LOCAL GOVERNMENT

Relationships between local government and the Scottish Parliament deteriorated somewhat soon after the elections to the Parliament in 2003. Although the Labour Party remained the largest party in the Parliament, it was weakened by the loss of eight seats and, in the coalition negotiations with the Liberal Democrats, it was forced to make a number of concessions. One of these, which was very controversial, was the commitment to introduce for the next local government election (due in 2007), the proportional single transferable vote system of election[40]. This system involves multi-member wards with populations considerably larger than at present. The proposal is controversial because it weakens the local member–ward link which councillors consider to be very important. Moreover, the proposal was made without prior consultation with COSLA, the body which represents much of local government. The 'single transferable vote' (STV) system with its multi-member wards is fiercely opposed by many councillors, particularly independent councillors in rural and Highland areas who value the local link, and also many Labour Party councillors who also value the local link but whose party benefits, particularly in the central belt, from the 'first past the post' system. A draft Local Governance (Scotland) Bill containing proposals for the introduction of STV for local government elections was put out for consultation in July 2003. At the time of writing, it remains to be seen whether the consultation process will result in a change of heart by the Scottish Executive.

There are three other commitments in the coalition partnership agreement which cause concern in local government circles because they appear to be areas where the Scottish Parliament and Scottish Executive intend to take powers away from local government. The first of these is the proposal to set up a Scottish Strategic Transport Authority which will have responsibility for delivering

---

[37] Eg the consultation process on the Ethical Standards in Public Life etc Bill resulted in the provision of an appeal to the courts against the findings of the Standards Commission.

[38] Bennett, Fairley and McAteer *Devolution in Scotland: The Impact on Local Government* (2002) ch 2.

[39] *Devolution in Scotland* ch 2.

[40] Partnership for a Better Scotland (2003) p 46.

concessionary fare schemes and for co-ordinating public transport across Scotland. Public transport is currently a local government function. The second is the proposal to establish a Single Correctional Agency which would remove from local government its current responsibilities for criminal justice social work services. The third issue is the proposal to extend ministerial powers of intervention to deal with 'failing schools'. Local government argue that specific powers of intervention in schools already exist but have not been used in the 23 years of their existence.

Local government members and officials have major concerns about the principle which seems to underlie these proposals, namely that if services need to be improved, they have to be put under central government control. They believe that this undermines the principle of subsidiarity which underpins both the Scottish Parliament and Scottish local government. The taking of local government powers by Ministers threatens the legitimacy of councils as the elected local leadership.

On a more positive note, the Scottish Executive has indicated that it will legislate to:

- reduce the minimum age for standing for election as a councillor from 21 to 18;
- increase the salary threshold at which local government employees become politically restricted and banned from taking part in many political activities;
- amend the law which requires local government employees to resign from their jobs as soon as they are nominated for election to the council which employs them;
- establish an independent remuneration committee and introduce severance and pension arrangements for councillors[41].

The Scottish Executive has also indicated that it will, at last, establish an independent review of local government finance.

As far as the public are concerned, the services delivered by local government affect them, literally, from the cradle (registration of births) to the grave (cemeteries and crematoria provision). Most Scots are educated in local authority schools, and many live in council houses. Leisure facilities, roads, refuse collection and disposal, and many other services impinge on the life of every citizen. What is important to the public is the efficient and effective delivery of these services and value for the money paid in council tax. The local dimension is also important: the delivery of services should take account of local needs. That is one reason why local government exists.

The old relationship between local government and the Scottish Office has changed with the establishment of a Scottish Parliament and a Scottish Government. It is important that the relationship between the two elected institutions is not one of rivalry, but of co-operation. The public will not be particularly interested in squabbles between the two, but may become disenchanted with both if the results are less satisfactory services. A covenant as suggested by McIntosh, adopted 'early in the life of the Parliament, and adhered

---

[41] All of the above were contained in the draft Local Governance (Scotland) Bill published in July 2003.

to by both sides', might well have put the relationship on a stable footing, but unfortunately that did not happen. The 'parity of esteem' recommended by McIntosh appears to be absent. Only time will tell if local government will survive in its present form and with its present range of responsibilities.

THE SCOTTISH PARLIAMENT AND OTHER PUBLIC BODIES

Despite the wide range of services delivered by local government, there is a huge range of public services which are delivered by unelected public bodies. Most of these are officially called Non-Departmental Public Bodies (NDPBs), but they are popularly known as quangos. They take a number of different forms. Some are advisory (such as the Scottish Law Commission), some have judicial functions (such as tribunals and the Children's Panels), some are regulatory (such as the Scottish Environmental Protection Agency), while others have executive functions and control large budgets (such as Scottish Enterprise, the Scottish Legal Aid Board, the Scottish Qualifications Authority and Scottish Water). Their members have been appointed by the Secretary of State for Scotland or, since July 1999, by the Scottish Ministers and there is no statutory requirement for any councillors to be appointed. There have been many criticisms of NDPBs, not the least of which are the lack of direct accountability to the public and the lack of transparency in the appointment of quangos members.

Prior to the establishment of the Scottish Parliament, the Labour Party in Scotland had called for 'a bonfire of quangos'. In the White Paper, *Scotland's Parliament*, the government expressed concern at the extent to which vital public services are run by unelected bodies[42]. Responsibility for all Scottish public bodies whose remits run wholly within devolved areas passed to the Scottish Parliament and Executive under the rules governing the Parliament's legislative competence (which have been dealt with above)[43]. As with local government, the Parliament is able to wind them up, alter their remits or merge some of them together. The Scottish Executive has taken over from the Secretary of State the powers to make appointments to their boards, to fund them and generally direct their activities. In 1999 there were 38 executive NDPBs and 56 advisory bodies and tribunals. Almost 3,600 persons were appointed to these (three times the number of elected councillors). They spent just under £2bn a year, while NHS health boards and trusts, which are not NDPBs but which are generally considered to be quangos and which have almost 350 appointed members, spent £4.5bn a year. Given the unique role of local government which stems from its elected status, the McIntosh Commission recommended that in any review of other bodies delivering public services, the option of transfer to local government should always be considered. Likewise, where new services are being developed prior consideration should always be given to whether local government should be the vehicle of delivery, subject to efficiency and cost-effectiveness[44].

The initial response of the Scottish Executive to McIntosh's recommendations was to confirm that, whenever a periodic review of a quango is carried out, the option of the transfer of its functions to local government would be considered as one of the options.

---

[42] Paragraph 6.7.
[43] See ch 2.
[44] The McIntosh Report, para 62.

In December 1999, it was announced that Scottish Homes would come under the direct control of the Scottish Ministers as a government agency. In February 2000, the Finance Minister announced a major consultation exercise on the appointment of members to quangos. The key objectives of the procedures for making public appointments system were[45]:

- to ensure public confidence in the appointment process by making it fair, open and transparent with appointments being made on merit;
- to be proportionate, ie appropriate to the nature of the posts and the weight of their responsibilities;
- to provide clarity and structure;
- to secure quality outcomes;
- to encourage a wider range of people to apply for public appointments;
- to be accessible and informative.

The Scottish Executive also wished to increase the number of women and people from an ethnic minority background on public bodies. In June 2001, the Scottish Executive issued a White Paper *Public Bodies: Proposals for Change*. In this, the Scottish Executive announced its intention to abolish 52 public bodies. However, closer inspection of the list revealed that only 11 were to be completely abolished. Of the others, some were to be declassified as public bodies, others (such as the three water authorities and NHS Health Boards and Trusts) were to be merged or reorganised, Scottish Homes had already been converted into an Executive Agency and was to be renamed Communities Scotland, while others were to have their status reviewed. Most of the bodies proposed for abolition were advisory NDPBs rather than the more controversial Executive NDPBs with big budgets and significant executive functions. There were no proposals to transfer quangos' functions to local government.

Some of the reorganisations and abolitions could be achieved by the Scottish Executive without the need for primary legislation while others (of bodies which had been set up by statute) could only be abolished by primary legislation. The Water Authorities were merged under the Water Industry Act 2002 and Communities Scotland emerged as a result of the Housing (Scotland) Act 2001. A miscellany of other bodies appeared as candidates for abolition in the Public Appointments and Public Bodies etc. (Scotland) Act 2003. These were:

- Ancient Monuments Board for Scotland
- Historic Buildings Council for Scotland
- Scottish Hospital Trust
- Scottish Medical Practices Committee
- Scottish Conveyancing and Executry Services Board
- Royal Commission on the Ancient and Historical Monuments of Scotland (RCAHMS).

As a result of successful lobbying, the Royal Commission on the Ancient and Historical Monuments of Scotland was removed from the list and survived the cull while the Ancient Monuments Board and Historic Buildings Council,

---

[45] Scottish Executive *Appointments to Public Bodies in Scotland: Modernising the System, Consultation Paper*, ch 2.

though technically dissolved, re-emerged as the Historic Environment Advisory Council.

The bonfire of quangos in Scotland has thus far not amounted to very much. The total number has certainly been reduced but some of that by what might be described as sleight of hand. Most of the executive quangos remain untouched and a few quite useful advisory committees have gone. The Scottish Executive has clearly realised, as have other executives before them, that public bodies have a role to play both in advising government and delivering services.

The Public Appointments and Public Bodies etc (Scotland) Act 2003 also provides for the appointment of a Scottish Commissioner for Public Appointments in Scotland whose functions are the regulation and monitoring of appointments to quangos by Scottish Ministers and the investigation of complaints arising from appointments.

It should be noted that the Ethical Standards in Public Life etc (Scotland) Act 2000 provides for a model code of conduct for members of the various devolved public bodies. The Standards Commission has powers to censure, suspend or remove from office a member who breaches the code.

CROSS-BORDER PUBLIC AUTHORITIES

Certain public bodies have remits which cover matters some of which are within the legislative competence of the Parliament and others outwith it. Such bodies include the British Wool Marketing Board, the Sports Council, the Advisory Committee on Hazardous Substances, the UK Live Transplant Support Service Authority, the British Tourist Authority and many others. These are known as cross-border authorities[46]. Scottish Ministers have the right to be consulted by their UK counterparts on the appointment of members and officers and on any specific function whose exercise might affect Scotland. The SA 1998 also makes it possible for the exercise of certain functions of cross-border public bodies to be transferred from UK Ministers to Scottish Ministers[47]. It is also possible for the Scottish Parliament to set up separate Scottish bodies to handle the specifically Scottish and devolved aspects of the cross-border authorities' work.

Some public bodies deal solely with matters which are reserved to the UK Parliament. These include the Equal Opportunities Commission, the Commission for Racial Equality, the BBC, the Post Office and the Benefits Agency. Although they deal with matters which are reserved, their activities continue to be of great interest to Scots. The Scottish Parliament's Standing Orders enable committees to invite the submission of reports and the presentation of oral evidence[48] to its committees. In certain cases, the Scottish Executive may be consulted prior to the appointment of chairmen or governors.

---

[46] SA 1998, s 88.
[47] SA 1998, s 89.
[48] Standing Orders of the Scottish Parliament, r 12.4.

11 THE SCOTTISH PARLIAMENT AND EUROPE

INTRODUCTION

Scotland, of course, is not just a part of the United Kingdom, but part of Europe. The issue of how the establishment of a Scottish Parliament would affect relationships with European institutions, and the European Union in particular, is one that was considered in the final report of the Scottish Constitutional Convention, and the government made various proposals regarding the relationship with the European Union in the White Paper, *Scotland's Parliament*[1].

The issue is important because the European Communities can and do make legislation which will be binding in all member states, or which member states are obliged to implement. If a member state has devolved certain of its powers to a devolved legislature (such as the Parliament), a mechanism has to be put in place to ensure that such a devolved legislature both implements European legislation which the member state is obliged to implement and also does not seek to make legislation which would contravene existing European law. Such a mechanism is important not least because the member state could in the last analysis be fined by the European Court of Justice, or be required to pay compensation to anyone whose interests had been damaged by a failure of a devolved legislature to comply with European law.

The reverse side of the coin is that it is only the member states that participate in the Council of Ministers, which plays the most important part in the legislative process of the European Communities (the only possible mechanism for formal participation in that legislative activity being through the minimal consultative rights given to regions in the Committee of the Regions). As a result, a devolved legislature will find itself being required to implement European legislation in the adoption of which it has had no direct say. It can readily be seen that such a situation, although perfectly feasible in terms of constitutional arrangements, is one that might present political difficulties both for the devolved legislature and the sovereign legislature of the state concerned.

The devolution scheme for Scotland addresses these issues in two ways. First, it incorporates mechanisms to ensure that the Scottish Parliament complies with European legislation and other obligations where these concern devolved matters. Second, it gives the Scottish Parliament some role in the European legislative and policymaking process, even although it is the UK which, as the member state, is the entity which has the right to take part in that process.

THE LEGISLATIVE PROVISIONS

The Scotland Act 1998 (SA 1998) seeks to ensure that the Parliament does not breach the UK's European obligations by means of a few simple mechanisms:

---

[1] Chapter 5.

First, it provides that any Act of the Scottish Parliament which is incompatible with the 'Convention rights' enshrined in UK law by the Human Rights Act 1998, or with EC law is outside the legislative competence of the Parliament, and does not become law[2].

Second, it provides that a member of the Scottish Executive cannot make any subordinate legislation, or do anything else, which is incompatible with the Convention rights or with EC law (subject to a reservation in respect of certain acts by the Lord Advocate relating to the prosecution of crime)[3].

Third, UK Ministers will continue to be able to implement EC obligations by means of secondary legislation, even where it covers matters which are devolved to the Scottish Parliament[4].

Fourth, the UK Parliament retains a general right to legislate for Scotland, even over devolved matters, and clearly this power could be used to ensure compliance by the Scottish Executive and Parliament with the UK's obligations under EC law.

Moreover, in the White Paper, *Scotland's Parliament*[5], it was envisaged that there might be cases where (with the agreement of the Scottish Executive) implementation of EU obligations affecting devolved matters might be achieved by UK (or GB) legislation rather than specifically Scottish legislation, and this has happened on a number of occasions. Furthermore, where EU obligations are to be implemented by separate legislation in the Scottish Parliament, it is stated that 'there will be arrangements with the UK Government to ensure that differences of approach are compatible with the need for consistency of effect, and to avoid the risk of financial penalties falling on the UK.' It can be presumed, therefore, if any concerns arising from such differences of approach cannot be resolved by agreement between the UK Government and the Scottish Executive, the UK Government may well use its reserved powers to legislate on devolved matters to resolve the dispute as it sees fit.

Accordingly, the legislation contains mechanisms to deal with any eventuality that might arise if the Scottish Parliament or Executive fails to comply with obligations under European law. An attempt to pass legislation or do anything which conflicts with such obligations is unlawful. If the Scottish Parliament or Executive refuses to legislate to take account of changing European obligations and as a result by an act of omission places itself in contravention of such obligations, the UK Government can enforce compliance by passing both primary and secondary legislation in appropriate terms. In addition, of course, the allocation of block grant is a matter entirely for the UK Government and Parliament, so no doubt any financial penalty falling on the UK as a result of such a breach of obligation could be compensated by a commensurate reduction in the grant paid to the Scottish Executive. (Furthermore, the concordat on EU policy issues, which is considered in the following section, commits the Scottish Executive to meeting the costs of any financial penalties imposed on the UK as a result of a failure on the part of the Scottish administration to implement EU obligations in devolved matters.)

---

[2] SA 1998, s 29.

[3] SA 1998, s 57(2).

[4] SA 1998, s 57(1). The power of UK Ministers to implement Community obligations by subordinate legislation is given by s 2(2) of the European Communities Act 1972 (see also Sch 5, para 7).

[5] Paragraph 5.8.

CONSULTATIVE ARRANGEMENTS

The requirement of the devolved Parliament and Executive to comply with European obligations is therefore clearly a cornerstone of the SA 1998. However, the Scottish Parliament and Executive are not given any statutory rights in the Act to participate in the decision-making process that eventually results in European legislation. This is in contrast with some other European countries, where devolved or federal regions and states have, in some cases, been given a legal right to take part, to some degree at least, in the process whereby their Member State takes part in the European decision-making and legislative process[6].

Instead, the UK Government proposed that a number of consultative, but non-statutory, methods should be established to allow the Scottish Parliament and Executive to play a part in those aspects of European business which affect devolved areas. This statement of intent was put into effect in one of the concordats agreed between the UK Government and the various devolved administrations after their establishment[7]. The Concordat on Co-ordination of European Union Policy Issues[8] states that it is the UK Government's wish to involve the Scottish Executive as directly and fully as possible in decision making on EU matters which touch on devolved areas (including non-devolved matters which would have an important impact on Scotland). It emphasises that such involvement by the Scottish Executive would be subject to 'mutual respect for the confidentiality of discussions and adherence by the Scottish Executive to the resulting UK line'. It indicates that without such respect and adherence it would be impossible to maintain such close working relationships, presumably implying that a Scottish Executive which refused to be bound by such conditions would be at risk of losing its right to participate in decision making on EU matters.

The concordat established a number of mechanisms to facilitate the involvement by the Scottish Executive in such EU issues. These mechanisms consist of the following:

- a commitment by the UK Government to provide the Scottish Executive with full and comprehensive information, as early as possible, on all business within the EU which appears likely to be of interest to it, with a reciprocal requirement on the Scottish Executive to provide information to the UK Government on such issues in its turn;
- access by officials of the Scottish Executive to the same relevant papers on EU issues as their Whitehall counterparts;
- reference of matters to the Joint Ministerial Committee[9] for discussion where differences between the Scottish and UK Governments cannot be resolved by more informal contact;
- the possibility of Ministers from the Scottish Executive attending meetings of the Council of Ministers on relevant matters, although it would be up to the relevant UK Minister to decide whether or not such attendance was appropriate. In certain cases, the Scottish Minister could speak for the United Kingdom as a whole, although the UK 'lead

---

[6] Eg, Germany and Belgium.
[7] See ch 7 for details of the concordats.
[8] Published as an annex in Cm 5240.
[9] See Ch 7, p 9.

minister' will retain overall responsibility for negotiations (similar arrangements would apply to allow participation in EU meetings at official level);

- the right of the Scottish Executive to establish an office in Brussels, for the purpose of assisting direct relationships with other European regional governments and with the institutions of the European Communities. Such an office is restricted, however, to dealing with matters which are within the competence of the Scottish Parliament and Executive, and is required to work closely with, and in a complementary manner to, the UK representation in Brussels. This qualification is clearly intended to prevent such an office turning into a 'Scottish embassy' or something similar, as advocated from time to time by the SNP;
- the delegation to the Scottish Executive of the appointment of the Scottish members of the UK representation on the Committee of the Regions, and the Economic and Social Committee;
- a commitment that the relevant Whitehall department would keep the Scottish Executive informed of EU legislative proposals, in order that the Scottish Parliament can, if it wishes, scrutinise such matters, and let the UK Government have its views on such proposals;
- detailed arrangements for ensuring that new EU obligations are implemented in Scotland as and when they arise, and for the co-ordination of the UK response to any proceedings taken against the UK for alleged breach of an EU obligation concerned a devolved matter.

It was emphasised in the White Paper, *Scotland's Parliament*, that the guiding principle on European issues is that there should be 'the closest possible working relationships and involvement' between the Scottish and UK layers of government, requiring the Scottish Executive to work in a 'spirit of collaboration and trust' with the UK Government.[10] Similar sentiments are expressed in the concordat on EU policy issues. At the end of the day, however, the concordat is not legally binding, but, as with all the other concordats, is intended to be 'binding in honour only'. Underpinning these statements of intent is a firm statutory framework to ensure that, at the end of the day, Scotland complies with EC obligations, either by the action of the Scottish Parliament and Executive, or, failing which, by the UK Government and Parliament taking steps to ensure compliance.

The experience of the first four years of the devolved arrangements suggests that these mechanisms have indeed worked reasonably smoothly, and more or less in the manner envisaged when they were set up. According to the UK Cabinet Office, information on EU events and issues reported by the UK Permanent Representation in Brussels ('UKRep') or by officials from Whitehall Departments is routinely shared with devolved administrations; devolved administrations are routinely consulted by the lead Whitehall Department on matters of policy formulation on European issues, and officials from devolved administrations will be invited to take part in UK-level meetings if there is a need to co-ordinate the UK line on a particular policy issue[11]. Scottish Executive Ministers do participate reasonably frequently in

---

[10] Paragraph 5.12.

[11] Memorandum submitted by the UK Cabinet Office to the House of Lords Select Committee on the Constitution's Inquiry into *Devolution: Inter-Institutional Relations in the United Kingdom*, HL Paper 147, July 2002, p 20, paras 49–51.

the Council of Ministers as part of the UK delegation, and on a few occasions the Scottish Minister has taken the lead on behalf of the UK as a whole[12].

The Scottish Executive established a European office very soon after devolution, in October 1999, sharing Scotland House with Scotland Europa, an umbrella body representing public, private and voluntary sector interests, which had already operated a Brussels office for a number of years. This office works very closely with the UKRep office in Brussels[13]. Working relationships have been set up between the Scottish Executive and UK Departments to deal with the question of whether European obligations affecting devolved issues should be applied in Scotland by the Scottish Executive or by means of a UK/GB statutory instrument[14].

The Scottish Executive has declared itself generally satisfied with the way that these mechanisms aimed at promoting co-operation between the UK and Scottish levels of government have worked in practice; and indeed, although the Joint Ministerial Committee on Europe has met on a few occasions to discuss EU issues and to review the co-ordination arrangements, it has so far proved unnecessary for the Committee to act as the formal forum for resolving any differences between the Scottish and UK Governments that cannot be resolved informally[15].

THE SCOTTISH PARLIAMENT AND EUROPEAN ISSUES

It is, of course, not just the Scottish Executive that has a role to play in European matters as far as devolved issues are concerned. Alongside the Scottish Executive's mainly informal role in the development of UK policy on EU matters has to be set the Scottish Parliament's role in this area. Given its legislative powers, the Scottish Parliament can decide how EC legislation is implemented in devolved matters (except in the unusual case of being overruled by the UK Parliament's reserved power of legislation). Moreover, although, as we have seen, it is ultimately the UK Government that decides what input there will be from the UK into decision-making and legislation within the EU, the Scottish Parliament decided from the start that it would take the opportunity offered to it of scrutinising EU legislative proposals in advance. To deal with such matters, the Parliament established a European (from 2003, a European and External Relations) Committee whose primary function is the detailed scrutiny of draft EU/EC legislation and its implementation within Scotland. In 2002–03, for example, the Committee considered some 900 documents relating to this area of its work[16].

---

[12] In the first three years from May 1999, Scottish Ministers had attended 28 European Councils, and taken the lead at three. See oral evidence given by Jim Wallace, MSP, Deputy First Minister, to the House of Lords Select Committee *Devolution* at p 166, para 563.

[13] Indeed, UKRep has been described as having a 'very close, even umbilical, relationship with the offices that the devolved administrations have set up in Brussels'! (Oral evidence of Stephen Wall, Head of the European Secretariat in the Cabinet Office: see House of Lords Select Committee *Devolution* at p 62, para 205.)

[14] See e g the working arrangements set out by the UK Department for Food, Environment and Rural Affairs in its Memorandum to the House of Lords Select Committee, *Devolution* pp 71–72, paras 18–22.

[15] See the Memorandum submitted by the UK Cabinet Office to the House of Lords Select Committee *Devolution* at p 20, para 53, and also the evidence of Jim Wallace, MSP at p 166, para 562.

[16] Annual Report of the European and External Relations Committee for the Parliamentary Year 12 May 2002–26 March 2003, www.scottish.parliament.uk/S1/official_report/cttee/europe-03/eur03-01-01.htm.

As well as its role in the scrutiny of EU legislation, the Committee was also given a remit to deal with 'any European Communities or European Union issue' and, since it was redefined to include external relations more generally, the international activities of the Scottish Executive concerning both the European Union and anywhere else in the world. The Committee therefore has the ability to fulfil both the specialist function of scrutinising EU legislation, and also the role of a generalist committee on European affairs. The Committee has enthusiastically taken up the latter opportunity, undertaking a wide range of activities ranging from major inquiries into aspects of European policy as relating to Scotland, submitting views on the proposals for a new European constitution produced by the Convention on the Future of Europe, the organisation of major public conferences, and the development of links with similar devolved parliamentary assemblies in other parts of Europe. It has also developed links with similar committees at Westminster and the Assemblies in Northern Ireland and Wales, particularly between the officials of the various bodies, with Members of the European Parliament from Scotland, and with the European Commission. The Committee appears, therefore, to be developing an interest both in wider European issues and contacts as well as specific European legislation, very much as suggested by the CSG in the proposals it made prior to 1999 for the way that the Parliament should operate.

As also suggested originally by the CSG, the committee refers matters as appropriate to other committees or to the full Parliament, from time to time. Much of the Parliament's work in the implementation of European legislation therefore falls to individual 'subject' committees of the Parliament. In addition, an important role in the process of implementing EU legislation is played by the Subordinate Legislation Committee, as subordinate legislation made by members of the Scottish Executive is often the mechanism by which such legislation is put into effect in Scotland. Overall, the arrangements made by both the Scottish Executive and Parliament for dealing with European business appear to be working in a satisfactory manner given the parameters of the devolution settlement. Certainly it appears that the Scottish Parliament European and External Affairs Committee is able to carry out a much more detailed and comprehensive scrutiny of proposed and actual EU legislation, as well as consider wider European issues, than its Westminster counterparts (which do, of course, have a much broader field to cover than that to which the Scottish Parliament is limited).

CONVENTION RIGHTS

As has been mentioned, the SA 1998 includes measures not only to ensure compliance with EC law, but also with 'Convention rights'. These are the rights laid down in the European Convention on Human Rights (ECHR), which the Human Rights Act 1998 (HRA 1998) has for the first time enshrined in UK law. Reference should be made to the HRA 1998 for the full extent of these new rights, but there are many devolved matters where it is easy to see how the Convention rights may have major implications both for the Parliament and the Executive. (As mentioned above, the HRA 1998 is one of the Acts of the UK Parliament which the Scottish Parliament is specifically prohibited from modifying[17].) For

---

[17] SA 1998, Sch 4, para 1. See ch 2.

example, the criminal and civil legal systems of Scotland have to be consistent with the right to liberty and security and the right to a fair trial, and must ensure that there is no punishment without law (which last provision prohibits, in general, retrospective legislation). Social policy has to comply with the right to respect for private and family life. Scotland already has experience of parents turning to the ECHR to vindicate their right to education in conformity with their own religious and philosophical convictions. Land reform must respect the Convention rights relating to the protection of property. This list of illustrative examples by no means exhausts the list of possible implications of the new Convention rights[18] for legislation by the Parliament and government activity by the Scottish Administration.

As legislation by the Parliament will be outside its competence if it is incompatible with Convention rights, the existence of such rights can give rise to challenges to its legislation both prior to Royal Assent, and thereafter. Similar challenges can be made to actions of the Scottish Administration if they are incompatible with Convention rights. As discussed above[19], the Convention rights were brought into effect for devolved matters in advance of their general implementation within the UK under the HRA 1998. By the end of 2002 there had been a large number of legal challenges made to actions of the Scottish Executive (and a few to Acts of the Scottish Parliament), the majority relating to the actions of the prosecution authorities, and usually relying on a claim that the Convention right to a fair trial had been breached[20]. Most were unsuccessful, but some succeeded, occasionally with major consequences for the criminal justice system[21].

The HRA 1998 also makes it unlawful for a public authority 'to act in a way which is incompatible with a Convention right'[22], unless the act in question is, in essence, based upon valid primary or subordinate legislation. (An Act of the Scottish Parliament will not be valid if it infringes Convention rights.) It is clear that under the HRA 1998, the Scottish Executive would be regarded as such a public authority, and almost certainly the Scottish Parliament also (as it is only the Houses of the Westminster Parliament that are expressly excluded from the definition of 'public authority'[23]). Any such unlawful actions by public authorities can be struck down by the courts, which can also award damages to the person who has suffered as a result[24]. To date, however, there have been no successful challenges to acts of the Scottish Executive or Acts of the Scottish Parliament under the HRA 1998, no doubt because most of the situations in which such potential challenges might arise will have to be raised as 'devolution issues' under the SA 1998, and cannot therefore be raised under the HRA 1998. However, even after the decision of the Judicial Committee of the Privy Council in *HMA v R*[25], it is still possible there may be situations in which an alleged breach of the HRA

---

[18] Schedule 1 to the HRA 1998 lists the 'Convention rights' enshrined by that Act.

[19] See Chapter 8.

[20] See Chapter 8, p 95.

[21] An early example of a successful challenge can be seen in *Starrs v Ruxton; Ruxton v Starrs* 2000 JC 208, in which the court held that a trial presided over by a temporary sheriff, whose tenure ultimately depended on the same person as the prosecutor, was not an independent and impartial tribunal. This challenge had major effects on the role that temporary sheriffs were able to play in criminal matters.

[22] HRA 1998, s 6(1).

[23] HRA 1998, s 6(3).

[24] HRA 1998, s 8.

[25] *HMA v R*, 2003 SLT 4.

1998 by the Scottish Executive cannot be raised as a 'devolution issue', and in those circumstances the aggrieved person will have recourse only to the remedies offered by the HRA 1998.

THE FUTURE OF SCOTLAND'S EUROPEAN LINKS

As we have seen, the Scottish Executive's current political majority has declared itself content with the current arrangements for participation by the Scottish Parliament and Executive in European issues. In essence, Scotland seeks through the various consultative mechanisms available to it under the devolved arrangements to ensure that its interests are represented within the global UK position in Europe; the absence of direct independent representation in Europe is compensated for by the fact that the UK, as one of the largest member states, has a larger influence in European decision making than Scotland could expect to have by itself. However, even the political majority which has led the Scottish Executive since 1999 has made efforts to increase its own direct representation within the European Union. This has included the establishment of a direct Scottish presence in Brussels, as described above, and the development of direct political links with a number of similar devolved administrations.

The Scottish Executive also decided that when the power to nominate Scotland's representatives on the European Committee of the Regions was transferred to it, it would share the places between itself and Scottish local government which had previously held all the places. It joined with six other European regions in a call for the Convention on the Future of Europe to give the Committee of the Regions powers beyond its current consultative role[26]. In its final proposals, the Convention gave short shrift to the idea of giving the European regions any greater power in European institutions. However, the very fact that both the Scottish Executive and Parliament see their involvement in Europe as going beyond a narrow concentration on the scrutiny of legislation, to the development of networks to give European regions a more direct voice in European institutions, may be very significant. It suggests that once the Scottish Parliament and Executive was set up, a dynamic began to work encouraging the development of a direct Scottish presence in Europe without the mediation of UK institutions – that dynamic had its effect even when the political majority in both the Parliament and Executive declared itself satisfied with the post-devolution arrangements for Scottish involvement in European issues. In the event of a government coming to power in the Scottish Parliament which was not so satisfied, it would not be difficult to imagine that the way that Scotland's voice was heard in Europe might be an early flashpoint of conflict with the UK Government and Parliament.

---

[26] The Convention on the Future of Europe sat in 2002–03 to consider revisions to the various treaties governing the European institutions, proposing in June 2003 a draft European Constitution. See http://european-convention.eu.int for details of its work. In May 2001, the Scottish Executive joined with Bavaria, Catalonia, North Rhine-Westphalia, Salzburg, Wallonia and Flanders in making a 'Political declaration' calling for a greater voice within European decision making for European 'constitutional regions' (see www.europa.eu.int/futurum/documents/contrib/dec280501_en.htm.)

12 RESHAPING BRITAIN

INTRODUCTION

The rioting in the streets of Glasgow and Edinburgh which greeted the announcement of the terms of the Treaty of Union in 1706 was not exactly followed by dancing in the streets on the passing of the Scotland Act 1998 (SA 1998) on 19 November 1998. Nevertheless, the Scots had turned out in considerable numbers to vote 'Yes/Yes' in the two-question referendum in September 1997[1] and the turnout for the first elections on 6 May 1999 was a respectable 58.2 per cent.

Perhaps not surprisingly, as the idealistic hopes of the supporters of a Scottish Parliament prior to its establishment were replaced by the experience of the raw politics of the new institutions, the initial enthusiasm for devolution waned somewhat in the years after 1999. Turnout for the second Scottish parliamentary general election dropped to just under 50 per cent, at 49.4 per cent, to the disappointment of the supporters of devolution (and to the glee of some of its detractors). It should be borne in mind, however, that the drop of just under 10 per cent in turnout between the 1999 and 2003 Scottish general elections was actually smaller than the drop in turnout between the 1997 and 2001 UK general elections, on which latter occasion turnout dropped by 12 per cent to 59.4 per cent. There is a strong case, therefore, that the drop in turnout for the 2003 Scottish Parliament elections was more to do with a general drop in participation in the electoral process (not restricted to the UK),[2] rather than any special features of either Scottish politics or the record of the Parliament and Executive. Opinion polls in Scotland have consistently suggested that support for the *principle*, if not the actual performance, of a devolved Scottish Parliament still runs at roughly the same levels as at the time of the 1997 referendum and the first election in 1999[3].

What can fairly be said is that there is little doubt that the Scottish Parliament is here to stay. All the political parties in Scotland now accept the fact of devolution to Scotland, even the Conservative Party which had steadfastly opposed it under the premierships of Margaret Thatcher and John Major. Indeed, some have argued that the arrival of the Scottish Parliament helped save the Scottish Conservative Party from extinction, with the Parliament's proportional electoral system allowing it to elect a significant block of members, giving it a profile which it had lost as a result of its loss of all its

---

[1] The turnout in the referendum was 60% – not as high as in the immediately preceding UK general election where the turnout had been 71.4%, but much higher than the turnout for local elections, which rarely reaches 50%, and on some occasions in recent years has dropped to as low as 20%.

[2] On the drop in turn-out in 2001, see Catherine Bromley & John Curtice, 'The Lost Voters of Scotland: Devolution Disillusioned or Westminster Weary?', in *British Elections & Parties Review*, 2003.

[3] See eg, the written evidence given by Professor David McCrone to the House of Lords Constitution Committee, HL Paper 147, pp 92–97.

Scottish MPs in the 1997 UK General Election. Meanwhile, the Scottish National Party has decided to work within the devolved Scottish Parliament in what it, at least, hopes will be the short-term while not relinquishing its long-term goal of independence.

Moreover, devolution to Scotland should be seen not in isolation but as part of the Labour Government's deliberate policy of decentralisation of government and as part of a wide-ranging programme of constitutional reform. The pace of reform has slowed since the early years of the Labour Government after 1997, but that programme of reform has already had major repercussions for the way in which the UK is governed, and is likely to continue to do so for many years to come. This chapter looks at that programme to date, and how it might yet continue.

DECENTRALISATION OF GOVERNMENT

First, the government's programme of decentralisation extends, potentially at least, to the whole of the UK, not just to Scotland. The Government of Wales Act 1998 established a directly elected National Assembly for Wales which assumed most of the responsibilities of the Secretary of State for Wales[4]. Unlike the Scottish Parliament, the Assembly does not have legislative powers, at least currently[5]. Its powers are administrative only, but there is a statutory duty placed on the Secretary of State for Wales to consult the Assembly on the government's legislative programme for Wales[6]. The Welsh Executive and the various subject committees do, however, have the power to prepare secondary legislation for submission to the Assembly for debate and approval, and this is a power which the Assembly has frequently exercised[7].

In the case of Northern Ireland, the Northern Ireland Act 1998 established (albeit rather precariously) a Northern Ireland Assembly. This Assembly has legislative and administrative powers. Like the SA 1998, the Northern Ireland Act 1998 adopts the retaining model for the distribution of legislative powers. In the case of Northern Ireland, however, in addition to matters reserved to the UK Parliament[8], there are matters which are excepted from the Assembly's legislative competence[9]. As a result of the religious and political circumstances of Northern Ireland, there are special provisions to ensure cross-community[10] support for various measures such as the appointment of the First Minister and deputy First

---

[4] Government of Wales Act 1998 (GWA 1998), s 22 and Sch 3.

[5] In July 2002, the Welsh Assembly Government set up the Richard Commission to consider, among other issues, whether the Assembly's powers should be extended. That committee was due to report by the end of 2003. See www.richardcommission.gov.uk for further details of the Commission's work. Whether or not either the National Assembly, which following the 2003 elections has a slim working Labour majority, would support any proposals from the committee for such a transfer of powers is an open question, as would be the attitude of the UK Labour Government, which would have to pass the necessary legislation at Westminster to make such a transfer possible.

[6] GWA 1998, s 31.

[7] GWA 1998, s 22.

[8] Northern Ireland Act 1998 (NIA 1998), Sch 3.

[9] NIA 1998, Sch 2.

[10] Cross-community support requires set percentages of designated Unionists and designated Nationalists to vote in favour of an issue.

Minister[11]. Furthermore, as a result of the political agreement which established the Northern Ireland Assembly and Executive[12], a number of institutions were established which provide for links between and among both the UK (and Irish) governments, and the devolved institutions within the UK. A British–Irish Council was set up which is comprised of representatives of the British and Irish Governments, the Scottish Parliament, the National Assembly for Wales, the Northern Ireland Assembly and the representatives of the Isle of Man and the Channel Islands. The council can meet at summit level, and also in special sectoral formats (which can be at ministerial or officer level) to deal with specific areas of policy. The council meets at summit level twice a year and on other occasions when appropriate. Its members exchange information, discuss, consult and endeavour to reach agreement on co-operation in matters of mutual interest within the competence of the relevant Parliaments and Assemblies. The elected institutions are also encouraged by the Belfast Agreement to develop inter-parliamentary links. Other institutions established as a result of the Agreement are the North–South Ministerial Council and the British–Irish Intergovernmental Conference[13]. Another related constitutional development was the Disqualifications Act 2000, the provisions of which allow members of the legislature of the Republic of Ireland to sit in the House of Commons and in the Northern Ireland Assembly[14].

England has not escaped the government's decentralising zeal. The Regional Development Agencies Act 1998 established nine regional agencies in England, all of which, with the exception of London, were operational by 1999. They have powers to further the economic development and regeneration of their areas, and promote business efficiency and employment in both urban and rural areas[15]. These agencies are quangos, their members being appointed by a Government Minister, not directly elected. In London, the government has established an elected Greater London Authority with a directly elected mayor and Assembly[16].

---

[11] Unfortunately, because of major disagreements between the Unionists and the Nationalists over the decommissioning of arms, the UK Government had to rush onto the statute book in February 2000 the Northern Ireland Act, which gave it the power to suspend the Northern Ireland Assembly and Executive. The powers were used to suspend these institutions on 11 February 2000 and, although the period of suspension ended on 29 May 2000, the government has now used these powers to suspend the institutions on three further occasions. Two of these were for one day only, but on 14 October 2002 a further suspension began which was still in place in June 2003. Indeed, the continuing political uncertainty led the UK Government to take the further steps of rushing through legislation to suspend the Northern Ireland Assembly elections due to take place on 1 May 2003. The first, the Northern Ireland Assembly Election Act 2003 suspended the elections for 28 days, but the second, the Northern Ireland Assembly (Elections and Periods of Suspension) Act 2003 allows for indefinite suspension, renewable by order every six months.

[12] The Belfast Agreement, also known as the Good Friday Agreement, made on 10 April 1998 as a result of the multi-party negotiations.

[13] The degree to which these provisions have been taken up varies. The Belfast Agreement (Strand 3.3) envisaged that the British–Irish Council would meet twice a year, and at other times when appropriate. In fact, it has only met about once a year, and up to February 2003 there had been only six sectoral meetings at Ministerial level. There also appears to have been very little activity undertaken to develop the inter-parliamentary links envisaged in the agreement (Strand 3.11). By contrast, by the end of November 2002, there had been more than 60 sectoral meetings held under the auspices of the North–South Ministerial Council. For details of the activity of these bodies, see www.british-irish. council.org and www.northsouthministerial.council.org.

[14] Interestingly, the provisions also allow them to sit in the Scottish Parliament and the National Assembly of Wales!

[15] Regional Development Agencies Act 1998, s 4.

[16] Greater London Authority Act 1999.

The Greater London Authority does not have its own tax-raising powers but raises revenue from precepts, road tolls and parking fees. The Mayor runs new transport and economic development bodies and has responsibility for attracting new investment, job creation and the regeneration of rundown urban areas. These are managed by the London Development Agency.

The constitutional developments in Scotland, Wales and Northern Ireland have acted as a stimulus for debate in England and in May 2002 the Government set out proposals for the establishment of elected regional assemblies, with executive and advisory powers, in those English regions where voters wished to have them. Mention is made above of the discussion within Wales about the possibility of giving the National Assembly some legislative powers, and if the English regions' demands were to go further and they aspired to assemblies or parliaments with legislative powers like those in Scotland and Northern Ireland, the UK might be set on a course which would lead to federalism. Certainly, in those circumstances, the role of the UK Parliament would have to be redefined.

CONSTITUTIONAL REFORM

Furthermore, the Labour Government's programme of devolution and decentralisation has to be set in a wider context of constitutional reform, much of which was set out in its manifesto for the 1997 General Election.

The European Convention on Human Rights has been incorporated into UK law by the Human Rights Act 1998, improving the access of UK citizens to the rights and freedoms guaranteed by the Convention[17]. Both the UK and Scotland have seen the passage of legislation giving citizens access to freedom of information, in the shape of respectively the Freedom of Information Act 2000, and the Freedom of Information (Scotland) Act 2002, although neither will be fully in force for some time.

In January 1999, the government issued a White Paper, *Modernising Parliament: Reforming the House of Lords*[18]. The first step was to legislate for the removal of the right of hereditary peers to sit and vote in the House of Lords. Before the year came to an end, legislation was on the statute book[19]. There is now a transitional house in which 92 hereditary peers sit on a temporary basis along with the life peers. An independent, non-statutory Appointments Commission which is responsible for identifying suitable Cross Bench[20] nominees and for vetting all the political parties' nominations has been established. The government also established a Royal Commission, under the chairmanship of Lord Wakeham, to consider and make recommendations on the role and functions of a second chamber and the methods of its composition. The Royal Commission reported in January 2000[21]. Its preference, in terms of composition, was for a chamber consisting of mainly appointed members with a small number of regional elected members. In response, the government published a White Paper, *The House of Lords. Completing the Reform*[22], broadly adopting the Royal Commission's

---

[17] See ch 11.

[18] Cm 4183.

[19] House of Lords Act 1999.

[20] Cross Bench peers are peers who do not belong to any political party.

[21] Report of the Royal Commission on the Reform of the House of Lords *A House for the Future* (Cm 4534).

[22] Cm 5291.

proposals, although with some important differences. Both the Royal Commission report and the White Paper, however, received a great deal of criticism both within Parliament and elsewhere. As a result, a Joint Committee of both Houses of Parliament was set up to bring forward further proposals. It produced its first report in December 2002[23], in which it set out a range of alternative options for the future composition of the House of Lords. However, in the ensuing debate, the House of Commons rejected every one of the seven options. In September 2003, the Government announced that it intended to proceed to remove the remaining hereditary peers from the House of Lords, with the remaining members to be appointed, although the possibility of further reform was not ruled out entirely.

Even the monarchy is considering how to modernise itself. The rules which govern succession to the Crown mean that male heirs and their children (regardless of sex) take precedence over female heirs, while the Act of Settlement 1700 and the Acts of Union 1706–07 confines succession to members of the Protestant religion and specifically excludes Roman Catholics and those married to Roman Catholics. These rules seem increasingly out of date in modern Britain and calls for the abolition have mounted in recent years. The Scottish Parliament has unanimously passed a resolution calling for the repeal of that part of the Act of Settlement which excludes Roman Catholics and those married to Roman Catholics from succession to the throne, but the UK Government shows little sign of making the legislative time available in the near future for the necessary legislation[24].

Changes to methods of voting are underway to increase the turnout at election. The Representation of the People Act 2000 aims to make it easier for certain people to register and to vote and allows for pilot projects of innovative electoral procedures in local government elections in England and Wales and also extended eligibility for postal voting in Scotland[25] as well as in England and Wales. The initial experience has been that election turnout can be increased substantially through the use of innovative methods of voting. In the local elections in May 2003, around 6.5 million people were able to vote by digital television, the internet, touch telephone, text message or by post. Political parties, which had previously been almost invisible in statute now require to be registered if they wish to field candidates at elections[26]. Restrictions have also been introduced on the sources of donations to prohibit foreign and anonymous donors and also on the amount of money a political party can spend in an election campaign and the amount spent by individuals or organisations in support of or in opposition to political parties. In addition, shareholder consent has to be obtained before a company can make a donation to a political party or incur political expenditure[27]. An important development was the establishment of the Electoral Commission[28], which is an independent body charged to oversee elections and the electoral

---

[23] HL Paper 17, HC 171.

[24] The process of reforming the law relating to the succession to the Crown is complex and legislating to change it would be a lengthy process involving the amendment not only of various UK statutes, including the Acts of Union, but also the statutes of the many Commonwealth countries of which the monarch is Head of State. The government has stated that repeal does not come high in its list of priorities.

[25] Representation of the People Act 2000, Sch 4.

[26] Political Parties, Elections and Referendums Act 2000 (PPERA 2000), s 22.

[27] PPERA 2000, Pts IV, V, VI, VIII and IX.

[28] PPERA 2000, s 6.

process, and make recommendations for change. It has stated its objective as being to 'gain public confidence and encourage people to take part in the democratic processes within the United Kingdom by modernising the electoral process, promoting public awareness of electoral matters, and regulating political parties.' Following the 2001 UK General Election, it undertook an extensive programme of investigation into numerous aspects of electoral law systems and processes, which resulted in the publication in May–June 2003 of a major package of proposals for further reform[29].

There has also been extensive reform of the voting system. The Scottish Parliament and the National Assembly for Wales are elected by the mixture of the first past the post and party list systems known as the additional member system[30]. The members of the Northern Ireland Assembly are elected under the system known as the single transferable vote. The members of the Greater London Authority and the Mayor are elected under a system called the supplementary vote, while the elections to the European Parliament in 1999 were on the party list system. All of these, to a greater or lesser degree, produce results in which the number of seats won by each political party is proportional to the number of votes cast for that party. They reduce the likelihood of one party winning an outright majority and thus coalition and inter-party co-operation becomes more likely.

The replacement of the first past the post system for elections to the UK Parliament could have wide repercussions for the way the country is governed. In December 1997, the government established the Independent Commission on the Voting System, chaired by Lord Jenkins of Hillhead. The Commission reported in October 1998[31] and recommended that the best alternative to the first past the post system would be a mixed system under which 80 to 85 per cent of MPs would be elected on an individual constituency basis, using a system known as the Alternative Vote, with the remainder being elected on a list system[32]. The government now appears to have little enthusiasm for changes to the electoral system for elections to the UK Parliament, but changes to the electoral system are still on the Scottish political agenda as a result of the agreement between Labour and Liberal Democrats following the 2003 Scottish parliamentary elections that the single transferable vote system would be used for Scottish local government elections[33].

Recent years have also seen a growth in the use of referendums at both national and local level. Until recently, referendums were used very sparingly by UK governments. In 1973, a referendum was held in Northern Ireland on the question of continued union with the UK. In 1975, there was a referendum on the question of the UK's continued membership of the European Communities. The implementation of the Scotland and Wales Acts 1978 was put to the people of Scotland and of Wales in 1979.

After the Labour Government came to power in May 1997, there were as many referendums in less than two years as there had been in the previous twenty-five. In 1997 the people of Scotland were consulted on the establishment of the Scottish Parliament and, separately, on the question of that Parliament having tax-varying powers. In the same year the Welsh were consulted on the establishment of the National Assembly for Wales. In 1998, the citizens of

---

[29] See www.electoralcommission.gov.uk for further details.
[30] See ch 3, pp 23–24.
[31] Cm 4090-I.
[32] Cm 4090-I, ch 9.
[33] *A Partnership for a Better Scotland* (May 2003).

London were consulted on the question of a directly elected mayor and an elected Greater London Authority, and the people of Northern Ireland were asked to vote on the Belfast Agreement. (The people of the Republic of Ireland were consulted in a referendum on the same issue by the Irish Government.)

Legislation is now in place[34] designed to ensure the fair conduct of referendums. It includes provisions for grants of up to £600,000 to campaign bodies, free mailing of referendum addresses and free air time for referendum campaign broadcasts. It also places restrictions on the publication and distribution of promotional material by central and local government and on referendum campaign expenditure by political parties. The Electoral Commission is required to be consulted on the terms of referendum questions. The government is committed to further referendums on a single European currency[35], and on devolution to the English regions[36]. A further innovation was the provision the government introduced (in England and Wales) allowing for local referendums on the introduction of a directly elected mayor in the local areas concerned[37].

As a result of the doctrine of parliamentary sovereignty[38], referendums are advisory only and cannot be considered as legally binding on the government or Parliament. Nevertheless, the government has regarded the results of the referendums held so far to be morally binding and a mandate for the actions they propose to take. Certainly, the SA 1998 had an easier passage through Parliament, in particular through the House of Lords, as a result of the overwhelming support for the Scottish Parliament expressed by the Scottish people in the referendum in 1997. As the British become more used to being consulted by government on major issues, there could, in the longer term, be implications for the sovereignty of parliament.

CONCLUSION

There is no doubt that for those who are interested in the constitution, these are exciting times. The establishment of the Scottish Parliament in 1999 led, almost immediately, to major differences in the way Scotland is governed. The question of independence for Scotland is unlikely to disappear from the Scottish political agenda, notwithstanding the success of the parties opposed to independence in both the 1997 and 2003 Scottish general elections. Although the SNP suffered a drop in support in the 2003 general election, the increase in support in that election for minor parties with at least a theoretical commitment to Scottish independence, resulted in the Scottish Parliament having more MSPs supporting independence after May 2003 than there were before.

For the rest of the UK, government has changed in ways that would not have been contemplated a decade or so ago. Notwithstanding the Labour Government's somewhat reduced enthusiasm for major constitutional reform, major changes are

---

[34] PPERA 2000, Pt VII.

[35] On 9 June 2003, the government announced it would be introducing legislation to allow for the holding (at some future date) of a referendum on UK membership of the euro.

[36] The Regional Assemblies (Preparations) Act 2003 sets out provisions under which referendums will be held prior to establishment of any such assemblies.

[37] Local Government Act 2000, Pt II.

[38] See p 8.

still on its medium-term legislative horizon – and one of the consequences of the changes it has introduced to date is that the course of further change is not now within Westminster's exclusive control. The constitutional map of the UK already looks very different from the way it looked in 1997, and it may well look even more radically different in the not too distant future.

GLOSSARY OF TERMS

Absolute majority: a number of votes which is equivalent to more than half of the total number of seats in the Parliament. The figure in a Parliament with 129 seats is 65 or more.

Advocate General: the Advocate General (for Scotland) is a Law Officer whose task is to advise the UK Government on matters of law relating to Scottish devolution.

Committee Bill: a Bill proposed by a Committee of the Scottish Parliament (rather than the Scottish Executive or an individual MSP).

Community law: the law of the European Communities, ie all the rights, powers, liabilities, obligations and restrictions from time to time created or arising under the European Community Treaties and all remedies and procedures provided by these treaties.

Constituency members: members of the Scottish Parliament who are returned by the first past the post method of election and who represent an individual constituency. In the first Scottish Parliament there are 73 constituency members.

Consultative Steering Group (CSG): a group which contained representatives of the main political parties in Scotland and others whose task was to report on the operational needs and working methods of the Scottish Parliament and develop proposals for rules of procedure and Standing Orders which the Parliament might adopt.

Convener: the person who chairs a committee. It can apply to a man or a woman and is therefore a better term than chairman.

Convention rights: the human rights set out in the European Convention on Human Rights, which have been incorporated into UK law by the Human Rights Act 1998 and the Scotland Act 1998. All legislation of the Scottish Parliament must be compatible with these human rights, as must, in general, be action taken by Scottish Ministers.

Court of Session: the highest court of civil jurisdiction in Scotland. Under certain conditions, appeal may be made from it to the House of Lords.

Declarator: an order of a Scottish court which declares the rights of a party.

EC: the European Community which the UK joined in 1973. The term EC law is the correct term for matters of law relating to the European Community Treaty.

EU: the European Union. Strictly speaking, this is different from the European Community and reflects a movement towards closer political and monetary union by the members of the European Community. The term EU is correctly applied to EU countries or EU citizens.

ECHR: the European Convention on Human Rights (now incorporated in the Human Rights Act 1998).

Executive Bill: a Bill proposed by a Minister in the Scottish Executive.

First Minister: The person who is the head of the Scottish Executive, normally the Leader of the political party with the largest number of seats.

High Court of Justiciary: the highest court of criminal jurisdiction in Scotland. There is no appeal from this court to the House of Lords.

Interdict: an order of a Scottish court which prohibits conduct.

Intra vires: within the powers of the Scottish Parliament as laid down in the Scotland Act.

Judicial Committee of the Privy Council (JCPC): a committee which consists of the Lord Chancellor, Lords of Appeal in Ordinary (the Law Lords) and all Privy Councillors who hold, or have held, high judicial office, together with certain distinguished Commonwealth judges. For the purposes of legal proceedings relating to devolution issues, the Commonwealth judges are excluded. In practice, the composition of the Judicial Committee of the Privy Council is very similar to the House of Lords when it sits as a court of appeal.

Junior Scottish Ministers: Members of the Scottish Parliament who are appointed to assist the Scottish Ministers.

Law Officers: in Scotland these are the Lord Advocate and the Solicitor General. The Lord Advocate is the principal legal adviser to the Scottish Government and is also the head of the system of public prosecution of crime and the investigation of deaths in Scotland. The Solicitor General is the deputy to the Lord Advocate. They are members of the Scottish Executive, but they need not be elected as MSPs.

Legislative competence: areas within which the Scottish Parliament can make laws as laid down in the Scotland Act 1998.

MSP: a Member of the Scottish Parliament.

Member's Bill: proposed legislation which is introduced by an individual MSP and not by a Scottish Minister.

Order in Council: a form of secondary legislation, made in a more formal manner than a Statutory Instrument.

Parliamentary Bureau: the PB consists of the Presiding Officer and a representative of each political party represented by five or more MSPs. There are also provisions for representation by parties with fewer than five MSPs. Its main functions are the organisation of the business programme of the Parliament and the establishment, remit and membership of the Parliament's committees and sub-committees.

Presiding Officer: the MSP who chairs the meetings of the full Parliament and is responsible for keeping order during proceedings in Parliament. The role is very similar to that of the Speaker of the House of Commons.

Private Bills/Private Legislation: legislation promoted through the Parliament, usually by bodies such as local authorities, occasionally by private individuals.

Quorum: the minimum number of members who must be present for business to be undertaken.

Regional members: members of the Scottish Parliament who are returned from the regional lists drawn up by the political parties or as individual candidates on the regional lists as a result of the second votes cast in the election. There are 56 regional members.

Schedule: part of an Act of Parliament which may be found at the end of the sections of an Act. It contains matters of details which cannot conveniently be included in the body of the Act such as the list of reserved matters in the Scotland Act. Not every Act has a Schedule. The Scotland Act 1998 contains nine Schedules.

Scottish Administration: this term covers the First Minister and the other members of the Scottish Executive, junior Scottish Ministers, certain offices such as that of the Registrar General, and their staff.

Scottish Constitutional Convention (SCC): a group consisting of members representing various political parties in Scotland (excluding the Conservatives and the Scottish National Party) and members from a wide range of Scottish civic society, such as the trade unions and the churches. The group produced various documents in which were laid out proposals for a Scottish Parliament. Much of the Scotland Act is influenced by their work.

Scottish Executive: the members of the Scottish Government, ie the First Minister, the Scottish Ministers, and the Law Officers.

Scottish Parliamentary Corporate Body (SPCB): the body which provides the Scottish Parliament with staff, services and property.

Secondary legislation: legislation normally made by Ministers which implements policy already agreed by an Act of Parliament or an Act of the Scottish Parliament. It is also known as **subordinate** or **delegated legislation**. The most common forms are **statutory instruments** and **Orders in Council**.

Sewel Convention and Sewel Motions: The Sewel Convention is the convention that the UK Parliament at Westminster will not normally legislate with regard to devolved matters in Scotland without the consent of the Scottish Parliament, even though Westminster has the power to do so. A Sewel Motion is the motion passed by the Scottish Parliament when it wishes to express its consent to such legislation by Westminster.

Standing Orders: the rules which govern the proceedings in the Parliament.

Statutory Instruments: one of the most common forms of secondary legislation.

Sub judice: currently subject to legal proceedings.

Subordinate legislation: see secondary legislation.

Ultra vires: outside the powers of the Scottish Parliament as defined in the Scotland Act 1998.

FURTHER READING

This section gives information about a number of publications which provide more detail of the issues dealt with in this book. It will be obvious that the list does not attempt to be comprehensive, but rather seeks to give some suggestions as to where readers interested in the subject matter of this book can turn for further reading. Most of the publications given below themselves contain references to further material on the subject.

Alice Brown, David McCrone, and Lindsay Paterson *Politics and Society in Scotland* (2nd edn, 1998: Macmillan). This book provides a comprehensive survey of politics and society in Scotland in the latter part of the twentieth century, in a longer historical context. It pays particular attention to the pressure for constitutional change up to and beyond the 1997 General Election. The book features an extremely comprehensive guide to further reading.

Noreen Burrows *Devolution* (2000, Sweet & Maxwell) This book discusses the general principles of devolution and deals with some of the legal issues which arose in introducing devolution into UK constitutional law.

Bernard Crick and David Millar *To Make the Parliament of Scotland a Model for Democracy* (2nd edn, 1997: John Wheatley Centre). The authors proposed draft Standing Orders for the Scottish Parliament, and many of their proposals were reflected in the final CSG Report. The authors also looked at the relationships after devolution between Scotland and Westminster, and between Scotland and Europe.

The Constitution Unit *Scotland's Parliament: Fundamentals for a New Scotland Act* (1996). This report examined the practicalities of the scheme for devolution proposed by the Scottish Constitutional Convention, and its work was influential in determining many of the details of the devolution scheme eventually adopted by the Government.

Report of the Consultative Steering Group on the Scottish Parliament *Shaping Scotland's Parliament* (1998: Stationery Office). The Scottish Parliament's Standing Orders are largely based on the recommendations contained in this report. It also contains useful appendices, dealing amongst other matters with equal opportunities issues, financial issues, and information and communications technologies. The report also lists (at p 91) various items of research commissioned and published by the CSG, examining in more detail some aspects of the operation of the new Parliament. The report is still a useful source of information, even though some of its contents have, of course, been superseded now that Parliament is up-and-running.

Michael Fry *Patronage and Principle: A Political History of Modern Scotland* (1987: Aberdeen University Press). A provocative, but thorough and valuable, history of Scottish politics from the 1830s to the 1980s.

Himsworth and Munro *The Scotland Act* 1998 (1999, W Green) This book contains the full text of the Scotland Act, together with extensive annotation and explanations of its provisions. It is a particularly useful volume for both students and practitioners.

James Kellas *The Scottish Political System* (4th edn, 1989: Cambridge University Press). Widely regarded as the standard textbook on Scottish government and politics. It provides a general historical and institutional analysis of Scottish politics, although obviously it does not cover more recent developments.

Murkens, Jones and Keating *Scottish Independence: A Practical Guide* (2002, Edinburgh University Press) This study looks at the steps that would require to be taken by a Scottish Parliament and government that wished to set Scotland up as an independent state, and looks at the consequences of independence for the Scottish people and the Scottish economy. In so doing, the book explores a number of fundamental questions about the Scottish constitutional settlement, and its relations with both the rest of the UK and the wider world.

Page, Reid and Ross *A Guide to the Scotland Act 1998* (1999, Butterworths).

Scotland in the Union: A Partnership for Good (HMSO, Cm 2225).

Scottish Constitutional Convention *Scotland's Parliament. Scotland's Right* (1995: Edinburgh). The final report of the Constitutional Convention containing its proposals for a Scottish Parliament, upon which the Government's proposals in *Scotland's Parliament* drew considerably.

Scottish Office *Scotland's Parliament* (1997, White Paper, Cm. 3658: Stationery Office). This is the White Paper that gave the details of the new Labour Government's proposals for Scottish devolution, which were placed before the electorate in the referendum of 11th September 1997.

Scottish Affairs. This journal is published by the Unit for the Study of Government at the University of Edinburgh. Since 1992 (and from 1977 in its predecessor *The Scottish Government Year Book*) it has regularly featured articles on all aspects of Scottish devolution, and Scottish politics in general. It also carries regular book reviews and lists of books received.

The Scottish Parliament itself has an excellent website (www.scottishparliament.uk) which provides up-to-date details of its legislative programme and the work of its committees, as well as general information about the Parliament and its members. Full details of the business discussed in the Parliament can be found in the pages of its website containing its Minutes of Proceedings and the Scottish Parliament Official Report. The Parliament's website provides a range of links to other websites concerned with aspects of Scottish government and public life, and to the websites of other Parliaments and Assemblies. The Parliament also produces What's Happening in the Scottish Parliament (published by The Stationery Office, for the Scottish Parliamentary Corporate Body, and familiarly known as WHISP), providing a regular report of its business and activities. The Scottish Executive also has a very useful website (www.scotland.gov.uk).

Stair Memorial Encyclopaedia: Volume 5, Constitutional Law (Reissue) (2002, LexisNexisUK) Parts 6 and 7 contain a wealth of material on the Scottish Parliament and the Scottish Executive. Part 8 deals with local government and the Scottish Parliament. Part 9 deals with judicial review of devolution issues.

The Stationery Office, Guidance on Public Bills; produced by the Clerking Services Directorate of the Scottish Parliament, mainly for use by MSPs.

Barry Winetrobe *Realising the Vision: A Parliament with a Purpose* (2001, The Constitution Unit) An evaluation of the first year of the Scottish Parliament.

INDEX